Leading Learning: Women Making a Difference

Leading Learning: Women Making a Difference

By

Lauren Stephenson, Barbara Harold and Rashida Badri

BRILL

SENSE

LEIDEN | BOSTON

The Library of Congress Cataloging-in-Publication Data is available online at http://catalog.loc.gov

Typeface for the Latin, Greek, and Cyrillic scripts: "Brill". See and download: brill.com/brill-typeface.

ISBN 978-90-04-37591-8 (paperback)
ISBN 978-90-04-37594-9 (hardback)
ISBN 978-90-04-37294-8 (e-book)

For family and to the friendships and collaboration that enabled this book to be dreamed of, developed and finally delivered.

∵

Contents

Acknowledgements

With respect and gratitude the authors acknowledge the five exceptional women leaders whose collaboration allowed this book to be written. The women are Raya Rashid (Um Dalmook), Rashida Al Badri, Rafia Abbas, Raja Al Gurg, and Fatma Al Marri. We are grateful for the time they shared with us to talk about their leadership and the access they gave to family members, friends and colleagues to add to the richness of their lived experiences of leadership. The support and friendship of the five women allowed the two expatriate researchers privileged insight into their lives and work which is highly valued and greatly appreciated.

The researchers also acknowledge the invaluable advice and critical overview given by Rashida Al Badri, who is both participant and third author. Her unflagging support of the research enabled us to keep the project moving forward through some challenging times.

Introduction

Women are the heart of the nation and integral to its progress. They're capable and empowered leaders who can take our nation to new heights.
H.H. SHEIKH MOHAMMED BIN ZAYED AL NAHYAN

∴

This is the first book that offers five narratives of the lived experiences of Emirati female educational leaders living in Dubai, United Arab Emirates. It is an authentic reflection of the educational environment in Dubai and the real-life experiences of educational leaders and teachers in complex leading, learning and teaching situations. Their different leadership experiences and practices offered through these narratives have the capacity to intensify the lived experiences of educational leaders and teachers and to transform the challenges of educational leadership practices in the region and beyond into meaningful individual and collective learning opportunities. The book comprises eight chapters:

Chapter 1 discusses the narrative inquiry methodology used in the ten year study. In contrast to traditional research, narrative inquiry is typically more accessible due to the ability of the researcher to tell engaging stories of the participants lived leadership experiences.

Chapter 2 provides an overview of the sociocultural context of Dubai and the United Arab Emirates (UAE) within which the participants' experiences occurred.

Chapter 3 presents a literature review which draws together key (educational) leadership theories and perspectives that resonate with the five Emirati women featured in this book and also necessarily draws on perspectives from the extensive leadership literature in other fields.

Chapters 4 through 8 present the narrated stories of each of the five participants, identifying key events and experiences that contributed to their leadership practice.

Chapter 9 presents the main findings, drawing together the key themes emerging from the stories to discuss the significant aspects of the participants' leadership practices and how these relate to the literature.

The researchers had privileged opportunities to talk not only with the participants but also family members, friends and colleagues and thus the narrated stories of the participants provide a rich insight to how their lives and work as leaders of learning developed over time. Through stories of lived experience, this book recognizes the expertise and contributions of these women to the fields of education and leadership.

This book is a significant text for both graduate and undergraduate classes in any courses where the professor wants to help students explore leadership practices and particularly through narrative means. It is appropriate for readers who wish to understand the practice of narrative inquiry as a means of exploring and accounting for natural phenomena. It is also suitable for anyone who seeks to understand the lived experiences of five female Emirati educational leaders and how their values have impacted their own leadership practices and those of others with whom they have worked.

About the Authors

Lauren Stephenson
Professor, Learning, Teaching & Educational Leadership, Faculty of Education and Arts, Australian Catholic University, holds a PhD in Educational Leadership from the University of Sydney and is an experienced educator with a background in teacher education, educational leadership and teaching English as an additional language/dialect (EAL/D). She has an extensive record of scholarly activities at national and international levels and has published in the areas of educational leadership, teacher professional learning, EAL/D, action research and narrative research methods.

Barbara Harold
is currently a Professor and Acting Director of the Center for Educational Innovation, Zayed University. She holds a PhD in Educational Leadership and Policy Development from the University of Waikato. She has had extensive experience in educational research for over 30 years. During this time she has undertaken individual and team projects and Ministry of Education contract research in New Zealand and the United Arab Emirates and has established credibility as a researcher with the local and international educational community.

Rashida Badri
until recently was the Principal of Greenwood Private School in Dubai and prior to that was Assistant Director of Dubai Education Zone for the private sector for many years. She has had extensive experience in private and public schools as an English teacher, supervisor of EAL/D teachers, and also as an administrator of Education affairs. She has a sound understanding of both government and private schools in the UAE and GCC region and has consulted and presented on educational matters at local and international conferences.

CHAPTER 1

Narrative Inquiry as Critical Social Research

> *Narrative inquiry is a gentle relational methodology that has the capability to uncover what is important to the person in their situation.*
>
> HAYDON, BROWNE, & VAN DE RIET, "Narrative inquiry as a research methodology exploring person centred care in nursing," *Collegian*

∴

This book is based on a narrative inquiry with five local women who have been involved in education, educational leadership and leadership in Dubai. Over a ten year period, we inquired into their involvement in education and their lives as educational leaders in order to make meaning of their lived experiences. In contrast to traditional research, narrative inquiry is typically more accessible due to the ability of the researcher to tell stories of specific events by using engaging writing techniques of fiction such as exaggeration, dramatic recall, and unusual phrasings to meet literary criteria of coherence, verisimilitude and interest (Richardson, 1999). The research has resulted in five narratives, one for each participant, which draw upon literary fictional writing and fictional ethnography (Ellis & Bochner, 1996; Rinehart, 1998; Sarbin, 2004; Trahar, 2009).

Narrative inquiry is an interdisciplinary approach to research, with its roots in various disciplines and philosophical traditions (Squire, Andrews, & Tamboukou, 2008). It is a methodology often used in education and sociology, however, the interest and use of narrative research within educational leadership is relatively new. "It is a gentle relational methodology that has the capability to uncover what is important to the person in their situation" (Haydon, Browne, & van de Riet, 2017, p. 1) and it enables the voices of those who may have remained silent (Trahar, 2013). It is the study of story, interpretation and discourse (Leggo, 2008) and "investigates what happened, the significance or meaning of that, and how it is told or shared" (Thomas, 2012, p. 210). As "a field in the making" (Chase, 2005, p. 651) it "is best for capturing the detailed stories or life experiences of a single life or the lives of a small number of individuals" (Creswell, 2007, p. 55).

Whilst there is scope for great diversity in the way that narrative inquiry is conceptualised and defined (Chase, 2005; Thomas, 2012), we understand narrative inquiry as both phenomenon and methodology (Clandinin, 2013; Clandinin & Caine, 2012; Clandinin & Connelly, 2000) that proceeds from an ontological position concerned with curiosity about how people are living and what elements make up their experience. It is a means by which we collect data about people's lives and collaboratively construct a narrative about the experiences and meanings they contribute to the experiences (Clandinin, 2013; Clandinin & Connelly, 2000). The stories lived and told are situated and understood within larger cultural, social, familial, intergenerational and organizational narratives (Caine, Estefan, & Clandinin, 2013).

> Through the stories common to the groups we belong to we create our familial, organizational, community and national identities. Our culture's "grand stories" teach us what "worthy" life is, what we should aspire to and what we should avoid, what is good and what is evil, what is forbidden and what is permitted. (Spector-Mersel, 2010, p. 208)

Narratives of experience work within the dimensions of temporality, sociality and place (Caine, Estefan, & Clandinin, 2013) and take into account the relationship between individual experience and cultural context. Narrative inquiry allows for an exploration of the social, cultural, linguistic, familial, and institutional narratives within which each individual's experiences were constituted, shaped expressed and enacted" (Clandinin, Caine, & Steeves, 2013) and as such is an effective means to structure beliefs and practices of educational leaders into meaningful units and make sense of their behavior and the behaviour of others. Just as these stories capture the experiences of individuals they also empower and allow the individuals themselves a more legitimate and authentic voice. Hearing the voices and stories of participants in the context of their own lives enables some deeper insights about the social and cultural contexts found within the field of educational) leadership in the UAE.

We chose narrative inquiry because of our interest in and appreciation of the participants' storied lives and the temporal nature of experiences. We were interested in the process and changes over time. We were also interested in the social dimension, the self, representations of the self and the concept of reflexivity, and awareness that the researchers are also the narrators (Chase, 2005). We did not observe the participants objectively; instead we took a subjective position in connecting relationally with the participants' social and private worlds (Clandinin, 2006a, 2006b; Pinnegar & Daynes, 2007).

Relevant ethical procedures were undertaken and approval obtained prior to the commencement of this study. The stages of this narrative inquiry approach involved the field, texts on field experience and the research text which incorporates the field and the texts and represents those issues of social significance that justify the research (Connelly & Clandinin, 2006). We drew upon Chase's (2005, pp. 656–657) five lenses:

1 Narrative is a distinct form of discourse
2 Narratives are viewed as doing or accomplishing something
3 Narratives are both enabled and constrained by a range of social resources and circumstances
4 Narratives are socially situated
5 Narrative researchers are narrators.

The narratives in this book were constructed using restorying which is a collaborative approach that involves the researchers and the participants in the negotiation of the final text. Because research drawing on narrative inquiry is life as it is lived (Phillion, 2002) narrative inquiry does not privilege one method of gathering data. We initially conducted intensive interviews with the participants and observed them in their workplaces and/or homes (Mishler, 1991). We asked questions that paid attention to: cultural context, beginning, middle and end, significance of other people, historical continuity, the embodied nature of the teller, and the choices and actions of the teller (Etherington, n.d.). We then triangulated the data sources in the following ways. We interviewed participants' mentees, critical friends and family members. Data were also collected through field notes, journal entries, documents, and artifacts. The participants' personal and cultural experiences needed to be taken into account within their historical contexts (Creswell, 2007). This inclusion of context is vital to enable our readers to understand and make sense of these narratives (Trahar, 2013). As such a rich description of the UAE context is provided in the following chapter.

Drawing on the narrative interview and other happenings, events and actions as a collaborative activity different co-constructed stories emerged through an interactive process (Chase, 2005; Trahar, 2009) where feelings, hunches and participant conversations were also woven into the stories (Clandinin & Connelly, 2000; Clough, 2002; Trahar, 2009).

As we collected the stories and descriptions of events, underlying themes were identified (Riessman, 1993, 2008) and synthesized into narratives co-constructed by the researchers and the participants throughout the research process rather than as a separate activity carried out after data collection (Gehart, Tarragona, & Bava, 2007). Therefore, the process of data gathering and analysis became a single harmonious and organic process in order to find narrative meaning (Chase, 2005; Etherington, 2003; Kim, 2016; Polkinghorne, 2007). Similarly to Sarbin (2004), we created fictionalized narratives drawn from memories and field texts composed and co-composed with the participants, and in response to lives and living. We then did a comparative analysis of the stories, identified themes across them and related those themes to the educational leadership literature. The participants' stories are at once unique in some respects and similar to other Emirati women's stories in other ways.

We therefore took a sociological and anthropological approach and based our inquiry on intensive interviews over several years about specific leadership aspects of the five participants' lives. We maintained long term involvement with this small number of individuals presenting the researcher/narrator and the researched (Tedlock, 1991) "together within a single multivocal text focused on the character and process of the human encounter" (Tedlock, 1992, p. xiii).

Narrative inquirers are cognisant of their audiences, that is, the participants and the readers, and as such we recognised that a story differs depending on the listener/reader and the teller, when the story is told and in what context (Mishler, 2004). As such our roles as researchers were complex and sometimes messy because of the level of human interaction and human relationship (Connolly, 2007, p. 453). Throughout the ten year process, we sought to recognise how 'race' ethnicity and other social differences are produced and as such we actively sought out and valued the nuances, complexities and richness that comes with narrative interviewing and narrative inquiry itself (Gunaratnam, 2003).

The idea that the researchers are the narrators "opens up a range of complex issues about voice, representation, and interpretive authority" (Chase, 2005, p. 658). The individual narratives in this book are presented as an "invitation to participate ... that ... may be read, and lived, vicariously by you, the reader (Connelly & Clandinin, 1990, p. 8). They are meant to be interpreted by you and you will hopefully derive your own meanings from the text. The researchers, however, assert an authoritative interpretative voice in Chapter 9 which draws together the key themes that emerged from the narratives.

We were interested in how the participants communicated meaning, how their stories were embedded in the interactions between researcher and narrator, how we made sense of participants' experiences in relation to culturally and historically specific discourses and how they drew on, resisted or transformed those discourses as they narrated their selves, experiences and realities (Chase, 2005, p. 659). We strove to attend to the ways in which the stories were constructed, for whom and why, as well as the cultural discourses that they drew upon (Trahar, 2009, p. 2).

1   Considerations and Challenges in Narrative Inquiry

Although narrative inquiry has become more widely used, it is also seen as controversial within the research community and has been criticised in relation to issues of subjectivity, reliability, validity, and generalisability. These issues along with ethical considerations are now addressed.

The issue of subjectivity has been raised in educational research literature (Coffey, 1999; Merriam, 1998). Case study has been faulted for its lack of rigor in the collection, construction, and analysis of data. This lack of rigor is linked to the problem of bias introduced by the subjectivity of the researcher and others involved in the study (Coffey, 1999) and these biases may not be readily apparent to the researcher (Merriam, 1998). According to Taft (1997), opportunities exist for excluding data contradictory to the researcher's views, thus important data may be overlooked. The authors addressed this issue through reflexivity, critical reflective practice and by fact checking and discussion of perceptions with participants' critical friends (Ellis, Adams, & Bochner, 2011; Etherington, 2006).

The authors believe perceptions and images that convey lived experiences in the past and present, and that anticipate the future, are open to different interpretations, just as is research data gathered in a more traditional way (Denzin, 2003; Denzin & Lincoln, 2003; Richardson, 1994). It is therefore important for the researchers to acknowledge their own biases, presuppositions and interpretations and analyse with those biases in mind. We therefore drew on strategies suggested throughout the literature for achieving credibility (Sparkes, 2002; Sturman, 1997), authenticity (Ellis, Adams, & Bochner, 2011), and fidelity (Blumenfield-Jones, 1995). These included explaining data collection procedures, documenting fieldwork analyses, reporting negative instances, distinguishing between primary and secondary evidence, distinguishing between description and interpretation, tracking what was actually done during different stages and devising methods to check the quality of the data such as conducting reliability checks (Ellis & Bochner, 2000) or cross checks with participants critical friends (Taft, 1997).

Qualitative researchers acknowledge their influences on those that they study and the importance of the role of knowledge generated closer collaboration with participants (Behar, 1996). For Ellis, Adams, and Bochner (2011) the concept of reliability in its orthodox sense does not apply in narrative. Similarly Freeman (2006) warns us against looking for a "validity" that encourages us to think that data can be confirmed by the speaker, where voice is considered representative and meaning as something that can be right or wrong. However, as Ellis and Bochner (2000) suggest, language is not transparent and one single standard of truth does not exist. Thus, narrative research should be regarded as valid within Ellis, Adams, and Bochner's (2011) definition which is that it seeks verisimilitude and it is authentic, lifelike, and possible (Polkinghorne, 2007). It is verisimilitude that the authors aim for in this book and the focus of generalizability is always being tested by you the readers as you determine if a story speaks to you about your experience or about the lives of others you know (Ellis, Adams, & Bochner, 2011). Narrative inquiry texts allow readers to interpret and focus on reference populations determined by the readers (Merriam, 1998). They may also extend readers' experiences by challenging or reaffirming their knowledge, skills and practices (Church, 1995) as educational leaders. In this book it is the readers who provide validation by comparing their lives to the narratives and by feeling that the stories inform them about other people or lives (Ellis, Adams, & Bochner, 2011).

Narrative inquirers are in a constant inquiry relationship with their participants' lives and cannot subtract themselves from relationship (Connelly & Clandinin, 2006, p. 480). In fact, what makes narrative inquiry unique is the acceptance of a relationship between researcher and participant during the data collection and writing phases. Both the researcher and participant are actively present in the narrative presentations (Haydon et al., 2017). Narrative inquiry accepts the influence the researcher (audience) has on the participants' narrative (Clandinin, 2006a, 2006b, 2013; Clandinin & Connelly, 2000). As such, narrative inquirers have relational responsibilities to the participants and negotiations of entry and exit, as well as the representation of experience, are key ethical concerns (Caine, Estefan, & Clandinin, 2013; Josselson, Lieblich, & McAdams, 2007). There needs to be both trust and openness in the research relationships, as well as reflexivity of the researchers throughout. According to Hammersley (1991), ethical considerations historically have revolved around five issues: participation, deception, privacy, consequences for others and for research. Just as in any research method these considerations must be addressed explicitly and transparently in narrative inquiry where honesty and high levels of ethical and critical engagement are essential.

A primary focus of narrative research is the protection of those who share their experiences, perceptions and stories with the researcher. However, the participants in this study specifically requested that they be identified by name. At the request of participants and with permission of those involved several family members,' friends' or colleagues' actual names were also included. Others were de-identified at the request of those involved.

Narrative inquiry then allows for the creation of a final product that is very different from commonly used methodologies in educational leadership encouraging more educational leaders to engage with this research. "These texts are intended to engage audiences to rethink and reimagine the way in which they practice and the ways in which they relate to others" (Clandinin, 2013, p. 51).

The participants' stories are significant in that they capture the lived experiences of five woman who made important contributions to UAE society at a particular time of change and development. There are few examples that record women's leadership at that time and significantly over a ten year time span. Furthermore, there are currently no known published studies that have drawn on narrative inquiry. We therefore hope that these stories will increase understanding and assist all educational leaders critically reflect on their own leadership perspectives and leading learning practices. The next section provides the contextual background to the participants' stories.

References

Behar, R. (1996). *The vulnerable observer: Anthropology that breaks your heart.* Boston, MA: Beacon.

Blumenfield-Jones, D. (1995). Fidelity as a criterion for practicing and evaluating narrative inquiry. *International Journal of Qualitative Studies in Education, 8*(1), 25–35.

Caine, V., Estefan, A., & Clandinin, D. J. (2013). A return to methodological commitment: Reflections on narrative inquiry. *Scandinavian Journal of Educational Research, 57*(6), 574–586.

Chase, S. E. (2005). Narrative inquiry: Multiple lenses, approaches, voices. In N. K. Denzin & Y. Lincoln (Eds.), *The Sage handbook of qualitative research* (pp. 651–680). Thousand Oaks, CA: Sage Publications.

Church, K. (1995). *Forbidden narratives.* London: Gordon & Breach.

Clandinin, D. J. (Ed.). (2006a). *Handbook of narrative inquiry: Mapping a methodology.* Thousand Oaks, CA: Sage Publications.

Clandinin, D. J. (2006b). Narrative inquiry: A methodology for studying lived experience. *Research Studies in Music Education, 27*(1), 44–54.

Clandinin, D. J. (2013). *Engaging in narrative inquiry.* Walnut Creek, CA: Left Coast Press.

Clandinin, D. J., & Caine, V. (2012). Narrative inquiry. In A. A. Trainor & E. Graue (Eds.), *Reviewing qualitative research in the social sciences* (pp. 166–179). New York, NY: Routledge.

Clandinin, D. J., & Connelly, F. M. (2000). *Narrative inquiry: Experience and story in qualitative research.* San Francisco, CA: Jossey-Bass.

Clandinin, D. J., Steeves, P., & Caine, V. (Eds.). (2013). *Composing lives in transition: A narrative inquiry into the experiences of early school leavers.* Bradford: Emerald Group Publishing.

Clough, P. (2002). *Narratives and fictions in educational research.* Buckingham: Open University Press.

Coffey, A. (1999). *The ethnographic self.* London: Sage Publications.

Connelly, F. M., & Clandinin, D. J. (1990). Stories of experience and narrative inquiry. *Educational Researcher, 19*(5), 2–14.

Connelly, F. M., & Clandinin, D. J. (2006). Narrative inquiry. In J. L. Green, G. Camilli, & P. B. Elmore (Eds.), *Complementary methods for research in education* (pp. 477–487). Mahwah, NJ: Lawrence Erlbaum Associates.

Connolly, K. (2007). Introduction to part 2: Exploring narrative inquiry practices. *Qualitative Inquiry, 13*(4), 450–453.

Creswell, J. W. (2007). *Qualitative inquiry and research design: Choosing among 5 approaches* (2nd ed.). Thousand Oaks, CA: Sage.

Denzin, N. K. (2003). *Performance ethnography: Critical pedagogy and the politics of culture.* Thousand Oaks, CA: Sage Publications.

Denzin, N. K., & Lincoln, Y. S. (2003). *The landscape of qualitative research theories and issues.* Thousand Oaks, CA: Sage Publications.

Ellis, C., Adams, T. E., & Bochner, A. (2011). Autoethnography: An overview. *Forum Qualitative Sozialforschung/Forum: Qualitative Social Research, 12*(1), Article 10. Retrieved June 9, 2013, from http://nbn-resolving.de/urn:nbn:de:0114-fqs1101108

Ellis, C., & Bochner, A. P. (Eds.). (1996). *Composing ethnography: Alternative forms of qualitative writing.* Walnut Creek, CA: AltaMira.

Ellis, C., & Bochner, A. P. (2000). Autoethnography, personal narrative, reflexivity. In N. K. Denzin & Y. S. Lincoln (Eds.), *Handbook of qualitative research* (2nd ed., pp. 733–768). Thousand Oaks, CA: Sage Publications.

Etherington, K. (2003). *Trauma, the body and transformation: A narrative inquiry.* London: Jessica Kingsley.

Etherington, K. (2006). Reflexivity: Using our "selves" in narrative research. In S. Trahar (Ed.), *Narrative research on learning: Comparative and international perspectives* (pp. 77–92). Oxford: Symposium Books.

Etherington, K. (n.d.). *A view of narrative inquiry* (PowerPoint presentation). Retrieved January 31, 2012, from https://www.keele.ac.uk/media/keeleuniversity/facnatsci/schpsych/documents/counselling/confeence/5thannual/NarrativeApproachestoCaseStudies.pdf

Freeman, M. (2006). Life 'on holiday'? In defense of big stories. *Narrative Inquiry, 16*(1), 131–138.

Gehart, D., Tarragona, M., & Bava, S. (2007). A collaborative approach to research and inquiry. In H. Anderson & D. Gehart (Eds.), *Collaborative therapy: Relationships and conversations that make a difference* (pp. 367–387). London: Routledge.

Gunaratnam, Y. (2003). *Researching "race" and ethnicity*. London: Sage Publications.

Hammersley, M. (1991). *Reading ethnographic research: A critical guide*. London: Longman.

Haydon, G., Browne, G., & van de Riet, P. (2017). Narrative inquiry as a research methodology exploring person centred care in nursing. *Collegian, 25*(1), 125–129. http://dx.doi.org/10.1016/j.colegn.2017.03.00

Josselson, R. E., Lieblich, A. E., & McAdams, D. P. (2007). *The meaning of others: Narrative studies of relationships*. Washington, DC: American Psychological Association.

Kim, J. (2016). *Understanding narrative inquiry: The crafting and analysis of stories as research*. Thousand Oaks, CA: Sage Publications.

Leggo, C. (2008). Narrative inquiry: Attending to the art of discourse. *Language & Literacy, 10*(1), 1–21.

Merriam, S. B. (1998). *Qualitative research and case study applications in education*. San Francisco, CA: Jossey-Bass.

Mishler, E. (1991). *Research interviewing: Context and narrative*. Cambridge, MA: Harvard University Press.

Mishler, E. (2004). Historians of the self: Restorying lives, revising identities. *Research in Human Development, 1*(1), 101–121.

Phillion, J. (2002). Becoming a narrative inquirer in a multicultural landscape. *Journal of Curriculum Studies, 34*(5), 535–556.

Pinnegar, S., & Daynes, J. G. (2007). Locating narrative inquiry historically: Thematics in the turn to narrative. In J. D. Clandinin (Ed.), *Handbook of narrative inquiry: Mapping a methodology* (pp. 3–34). Thousand Oaks, CA: Sage Publications.

Polkinghorne, D. E. (2007). Validity issues in narrative research. *Qualitative Inquiry, 13*(4), 471–486.

Richardson, L. (1994). Writing: A method of inquiry. In N. K. Denzin & Y. S. Lincoln (Eds.), *Handbook of qualitative research* (pp. 516–529). Thousand Oaks, CA: Sage Publications.

Richardson, L. (1999). Feathers in our cap. *Journal of Contemporary Ethnography, 28*(6), 660–668.

Riessman, C. K. (1993). *Narrative analysis*. Newbury Park, CA: Sage Publications.

Riessman, C. K. (2008). *Narrative methods for the human sciences*. Thousand Oaks, CA: Sage Publications.

Rinehart, R. (1998). Fictional methods in ethnography: Believability, specks of glass, and Chekhov. *Qualitative Inquiry, 4*(2), 200–224.

Sarbin, T. (2004). The role of imagination in narrative construction. In C. Daiute & C. Lightfoot (Eds.), *Narrative analysis: Studying the development of individuals in society* (pp. 5–20). Thousand Oaks, CA: Sage Publications.

Sparkes, A. C. (2002). Autoethnography: Self-indulgence or something more? In A. Bochner & C. Ellis (Eds.), *Ethnographically speaking: Autoethnography, literature, and aesthetics.* New York, NY: Rowman & Littlefield.

Spector-Mersel, G. (2010). Narrative research: Time for a paradigm. *Narrative Inquiry, 20*(1), 204–224. doi:10.1075/ni.20.1.10spe

Squire, C., Andrews, M., & Tamboukou, M. (2008). What is narrative research? In M. Andrews, C. Squire, & M. Tamboukou (Eds.), *Doing narrative research* (pp. 1–19). London: Sage Publications.

Sturman, A. (1997). Case study methods. In J. P. Keeves (Ed.), *Educational research, methodology and measurement: An international handbook* (2nd ed., pp. 61–66). Oxford: Pergamon.

Taft, R. (1997). Ethnographic research methods. In J. P. Keeves (Ed.), *Educational research, methodology, and measurement: An international handbook* (2nd ed.). Cambridge: CUP.

Tedlock, B. (1991). From participant observation to the observation of participation: The emergence of narrative ethnography. *Journal of Anthropological Research, 47,* 69–94.

Tedlock, B. (1992). *The beautiful and the dangerous: Encounters with the Zuni Indians.* New York, NY: New Press.

Thomas, S. (2012). Narrative inquiry: Embracing the possibilities. *Qualitative Research Journal, 12*(2), 206–221. https://doi.org/10.1108/14439881211248356

Trahar, S. (2009). Beyond the story itself: Narrative inquiry and autoethnography in intercultural research in higher education. *Forum Qualitative Sozialforschung/ Forum: Qualitative Social Research, 10*(1), Article 30. Retrieved from http://nbn-resolving.de/urn:nbn:de:0114-fqs0901308

Trahar, S. (2013). *Contextualising narrative inquiry: Developing methodological approaches for local contexts.* Hoboken, NJ: Taylor and Francis.

CHAPTER 2

Contextual Background of the United Arab Emirates (UAE)

Dubai is a stirring alchemy of profound traditions and ambitious futuristic vision wrapped into starkly evocative desert splendour.
ANONYMOUS

∴

To fully understand the themes within the participants' stories it is important to understand the context in which these took place. Foremost in the context is an understanding of the Islamic roots that underpin the participants' world view. Islam is inextricably interwoven into the everyday life of Muslim women, playing a key role in how they construct their identities of self. The values of modesty, humility, service to others, credibility, caring for family and the daily practices and rituals of Islam underpin the participants' stories.

The span of time of participants' stories covered the 1950s to the present. During that period the UAE went through some dramatic changes in education, the socioeconomic sector and governance. Prior to Federation in 1971 the current UAE comprised separate emirates and was known as the Trucial States. The population was centered either in larger coastal towns such as Dubai and Abu Dhabi or in smaller villages in the oases and mountain regions. Economic activity in the urban areas was mainly centered around agriculture, pearl diving, fishing and mercantile/trading activity. Social life was dominated by a tribal system with well structured social hierarchies and kinship structures. There was no formal education system prior to 1953 when the first boys' school opened in Sharjah emirate but children (boys) from wealthy families were often sent abroad for their education. During this period local children were educated by 'mutawa'a,' respected local men and women who taught groups of children in their homes. The mutawa'a taught youngsters to read Arabic through studying and memorising the Holy Quran. The mutawa'a was also responsible for reinforcing moral obligations and understanding of Islamic practices and obligations and was held in high esteem as a wise and respectable member of the community (Alhebsi, Pettaway, & Waller, 2015). This was the era that Raya grew up in. Even up to the 70 s it was still common for parents to send their sons and daughters to local 'mutawa'a' in the long summer holidays.

Between 1953 and Federation in 1971 the number of public schools and educational institutions began to grow. Initially they were funded from outside the UAE by counties such as Kuwait, Bahrain, Qatar, Saudi Arabia and Egypt who also sent expatriate teachers and curriculum to support the education system. Some Emirati teachers entered the profession in Dubai and Sharjah in the late 60 s, graduating from the Sharjah Institute of Education.

The key impact on Emirati society in that time was the discovery of oil in Abu Dhabi in 1962 and then in Dubai in 1969 which brought unprecedented wealth and economic development. H.H. Sheikh Zayed bin Sultan Al Nahayan became Ruler of Abu Dhabi in 1966 and immediately began channeling the oil revenues into roads, schools, hospitals and housing.

H.H. Sheikh Zayed also led the next key development that was the change from seven individual emirates into the Federation in 1971 that was the formation of the current UAE. The leadership of those 'founding fathers' and of H.H. Sheikh Zayed in particular was visionary and forward thinking reflecting tribal cultural norms of caring for and supporting one's own. Members of the community were energized and motivated by this leadership to take part in the development of their country. H.H. Sheikh Zayed led the UAE until his death in 2004 and today is still revered as the 'father of the nation' whose leadership philosophy and practices are emulated by Emiratis across all sectors of society.

After Federation in 1971 the UAE gradually regained control of its own education system with the establishment of the Ministry of Education in 1972. Expatriate Arab teachers were still employed (although decreasing in number) in girls' schools (e.g. to teach French) and were often very competent in their subject areas having been educated in other universities. Boys' schools still relied heavily on expatriate Arab teachers but as the higher education system began to develop, increasing numbers of Emirati females began to move into teaching. This movement was aided by the opening of the national United Arab Emirates University in 1976, Higher Colleges of Technology in 1988 and Zayed University in 1998, each of which had teacher education programs.

1   The Educational Context

From the Federation of the Emirates emerged a new sense of national unity and a strong desire to contribute to and build Emirati society. The developing education system opened up new opportunities for young nationals. The UAE

University (UAEU), for example, had segregated residential facilities that made it easier for a wider range of students to attend. The idea of sending their daughters outside the home during the week to university dormitories was something new and strange to families yet they supported this initiative, taking their daughters to the bus station at the beginning of each week then picking them up again at the weekend. In those early days there were no mobile phones and one public phone in the UAEU dormitories. However, the government encouraged families to send their daughters for higher education studies and there was a high degree of trust among families that their daughters would be secure and safe. Students returned home for weekends and summer and other holidays.

Although national institutions were becoming well established it was still common for young adults from families with wealth or position to travel abroad for their tertiary education to Kuwait or other Gulf countries, or to the UK and USA. It was not an easy step for families to send daughters abroad and yet, as within the UAE, they supported higher education opportunities.

During the 1980s large numbers of young women started in the paid workforce, the majority of whom went into the field of education. There was strong support for the government at that time to send Emirati teachers overseas to participate in conferences and seminars and to bring back new ideas and content with which the UAE could begin to set up its own educational conferences. In this way fresh ideas and educational approaches permeated the developing education system.

What was at that time (and still is) distinctive about the UAE is its views about the importance of education for both males and females, exemplified in the quote by H.H. the late Sheikh Zayed:

> The real asset of any advanced nation is its people, especially the educated ones, and the prosperity and success of the people are measured by the standard of their education. ("Shaikh Zayed in quotes," 2005, October 31, para 18)

2   The Family Context

Prior to federation and the discovery of oil family life in the UAE was characterized by 'big' families where grandparents, parents, aunts and uncles and children lived and socialized closely together. Family members would have rooms in the same house, coming together to share meals (up to the 1960s men would eat separately to women and children). These family patterns started to change in the 1970s when the government gave land and money for houses and the larger families started to morph into smaller family units living in their own homes. However, the 'big' family continued to come together on the weekends to meet and share meals.

For our participants who were university students during the 70 s the weekends were a time to enjoy a break from hostel life, to spend time with family and to visit relatives, especially older family members. During the long summer break, some girls, with family approval and support, would travel overseas to visit foreign countries where they could practice their English. Others worked during this time; for example teaching the Holy Quran to young people, which was an initiative supported by the then President, H.H. Sheikh Zayed.

Another popular family activity was desert camping when the weather was suitable. They would build areesh (dwellings) of date palm fronds that would allow natural air conditioning as the wind blew through gaps in the fronds. The desert lifestyle was relaxed and children would amuse themselves by rolling down the sand dunes.

3   Women's Leadership in the UAE

Throughout the greater part of the twentieth century women's leadership was predominantly played out in the home and family and, for some as noted earlier, in the support of education. Following Federation, H.H. Sheikha Fatima bint Mubarak, the wife of H.H. the late Sheikh Zayed, established the General Women's Union (GWU) as a strategy to bring all women's associations in the UAE under one 'umbrella' group to more effectively further women's socioeconomic progress. Still active both locally, regionally and internationally, the GWU has spearheaded many advances for UAE women in the social sphere. H.H. Sheikha Fatima remains a powerful and respected leader in women's affairs and has just recently also launched the Strategy for the Empowerment of Emirati Women 2015–2021. In 2006, H.H. Sheikha Manal bint Mohamed bin Rashid Al Maktoum initiated the Dubai Women Establishment (DWE). One of its early initiatives was a UAE Women's Leadership program to support professional learning and build the leadership capacity of Emirati women leaders.

4   Leadership in Business

Leadership opportunities for women have also been available in business and commerce. These opportunities have increased dramatically in the last decade following the establishment of the UAE Business Women Council in 2002, an organization that now comprises over 12,000 members. Allied Business Women organizations in Dubai and Abu Dhabi have been active in organizing local professional learning and entrepreneurship opportunities and global conferences and symposia. Currently, more than ten thousand businesswomen in the country own and run their own businesses. One such business woman is H.H. Sheikha Lubna who is an example of how far Emirati women can rise in this sector. Beginning her career as a software programmer in 1981 she moved rapidly to become senior manager at the Dubai Ports Authority. Her leadership skills were noticed by H.H. Sheikh Mohammad, ruler of Dubai and she obtained several further prominent positions before being appointed as Minister of Economic and Planning in 2000. In 2004 she was appointed as Minister of Foreign Trade. One of the participants, Raja Al Gurg, is another example of a highly esteemed Dubai woman leading a business which is spread across the UAE, Oman, Saudi Arabia and Iraq, with 48 nationalities and close to 3000 employees.

5   Leadership in Politics

H.H. Sheikha Lubna crossed from the world of commerce into the world of politics and in the last decade this is another field in which Emirati women have distinguished themselves. The Federal National Council (FNC) was inaugurated in 1971. This advisory body to the UAE government allows Emirati citizens a voice at the higher levels of national decision making. The year 2006 was an historic one for women where nine became members of the FNC. Significantly, one of the participants, Fatma Al Marri was elected at this time. In 2011, eighty five out of four hundred and sixty eight candidates standing for election were women. In the most recent election in 2015 women claimed another historic milestone when Dr Amal Qbaisi was appointed as the first women Speaker in the UAE and Arab world.

6   Conclusion

The context of the participants' stories is the UAE emirate of Dubai and their narratives took place during a time of rapid socioeconomic and political change as the UAE emerged from a modest economic system to become a global hub. Following the discovery of oil, and Federation, UAE's rulers, notably the late Sheikh Zayed, focused on nation building for the betterment of their people, while welcoming expatriate contributions to economic development. Their style of leadership that was inclusive, supportive and forward thinking laid the groundwork for Emirati citizens to also lead and contribute to their country's development. It is within this changing context that our participants' stories are framed.

References

Alhebsi, A., Pettaway, L. D., & Waller, L. (2015). A history of education in the United Arab Emirates and Trucial Sheikdoms. *The Global e-Learning Journal, 4*(1), 1–8.

Shaikh Zayed in quotes. (2005, October 31). *Gulf News*. Retrieved from http://gulfnews.com/news/uae/general/shaikh-zayed-in-quotes-1.306268

CHAPTER 3

Perspectives on Leadership

∤

Be a lamp, or a lifeboat, or a ladder. Help someone's soul heal. Walk out
of your house like a shepherd.
RUMI

∴

1   Introduction

In recent years there has been an ever-increasing focus on the nature and
importance of women's leadership in education in the UAE and in Dubai in
particular. As evidence of this, consider the various leadership certificates,
programs, symposia, conferences, workshops, degrees and awards currently
offered in the region with an emphasis on educational administration
and leadership. This chapter draws together key leadership theories
and perspectives that resonate with the five Emirati women featured in
this book and also necessarily draws on perspectives from the extensive
leadership literature in other fields. Leadership perspectives tend to focus
on cognitive, emotional, spiritual and behavioural aspects; however, there
is still no consensus on the meaning of leadership. The authors concur with
Northouse's (2007, p. 3) definition that "Leadership is a process whereby
an individual influences a group of individuals to achieve a common goal."
This chapter suggests a multidimensional leadership approach with a focus
on situational, transformational, servant, shared and positive leadership
perspectives. Given the ever increasing important focus of educational leaders
"on learning, the central and unique purpose of educational organizations"
(Bush & Glover, 2014, p. 564), leading learning and teaching is also necessarily
emphasized. Furthermore, like Shah (2016), the authors advocate for the
need to move beyond the mainstream educational leadership which has
been predominantly informed by Western ideologies, concepts, theories
and practices (Dimmock, 2000, 2002) to an understanding of (educational)
leadership formulated in context and from a cultural and Islamic perspective
(Shah, 2006). At times these perspectives have overlapped, influenced each
other or run parallel (Bush & Glover, 2014). The primary aim of this chapter

is to set up a framework of perspectives useful for understanding educational leadership in the UAE and is subsequently used in the analysis of participants' narratives.

The literature typically examines these perspectives as either ways to understand, and analyse educational leadership practices or as recommended preferred approaches to educational leadership (Bush, 2011; Bush & Glover, 2014). Transformational, instructional and shared leadership perspectives have been strongly advocated with sometimes limited evidence to support such claims. The authors suggest that effective educational leaders choose the most appropriate style grounded in context and each situational event or challenge. By drawing from such diverse perspectives we aim to examine notions of women leading learning, the changing Dubai context and increase understanding of leadership concepts and practices within the region.

2   Situational Leadership

Situational leadership is a democratic leadership perspective that advocates inclusion, participation and consultation (Starrat, 2001). It suggests that there is no one best leadership style for all situations but rather, leaders should remain flexible in order to meet the changing needs of context and situation. It is concerned with leadership as a process and the interaction between leadership and context. A situational leader can apply what he or she knows to different situations to influence others.

Hersey and Blanchard (1993) argue that a person's leadership style must be flexible enough to meet the changing needs of organisational members and the situation. Their framework is based on the amount of direction (task behavior) and the amount of socio-emotional support (relationship behavior) a leader must provide within the context. At the same time, the amount of either relationship or task behaviour is dependent on the readiness of the follower. Task behaviour can be considered directive and refers to the control and supervision leaders use with their followers. Relationship behaviour can be considered people oriented and is considered supportive. It refers to a leaders' listening skills (Morrison, 1994), the support they provide followers and the extent to which followers are involved in decision-making. Follower readiness refers to the followers' willingness and ability to perform tasks. These two dimensions of leadership behavior (directive and supportive) can be plotted on two distinct axes to form four leadership styles that differ in the amount of direction, support, and encouragement the leader provides and the amount of follower involvement in decision making (Carew, Parisi-Carew, & Blanchard, 1986). The four different types of situational leadership are directing, coaching, supporting and delegating. Depending on the level of these variables, leaders must apply the most appropriate leadership style to fit the given situation. The three steps of situational leadership are:

1 Identify the most important tasks or priorities
2 Diagnose the readiness level of the followers
3 Decide the matching leadership style/practice

From this perspective then, the most effective leaders are those who are flexible and capable of using different leadership styles and approaches to meet the demands of the situation and the varying maturity levels of their followers.

3   Transformational Leadership

Transformational leadership provides a normative approach to leadership and largely focuses on the process by which leaders seek to influence outcomes rather than the nature or direction of those outcomes (Bush, 2003; Burns, 1978). Authentic transformational leadership builds genuine trust between leaders and followers and typically makes a positive impact on motivation, empowerment and morality of organisational members (Begley, 2006; Gill, 2006). This should not be confused with 'pseudo-transformational leadership' (Bass, 1997) which has been criticised as being a political rather than collegial leadership approach where the leader's own (sometimes questionable) values, and strong, heroic and charismatic features can manipulate others (Allix, 2000; Bass & Avolio, 1994; Conger, 1990).

The main goal of transformational leadership is to gain the support of followers toward a common, legitimate organisational goal (Bass, 1990; Lynch, 2012) as a result of the followers' acceptance of certain values that the leader espouses (Wofford et al., 2001). Just as charismatic leaders do, transformational leaders transform followers' thoughts and attitudes motivating them to perform beyond expectations. Transformational leaders prefer to develop personal relationships with their followers by dealing with them individually instead of in group settings. The social aspect of educational leadership is vested in sequences of collaboration and communication between individuals (Bourdieu, 1984). Transformational leaders use consultative and participative styles which naturally allow the followers to feel more valued and appreciated, thus building confidence resulting in greater risk taking (Lynch, 2012).

Transformational leaders aim to develop a work culture that instils a sense of belonging among the followers which in turn fosters a sense of shared vision (Lynch, 2012).

Transformational leadership is a collegial model and emphasises that when followers identify with a leader and the leader's vision, they feel a sense of empowerment, and work together to achieve the vision. Furthermore, transformational leaders encourage their followers to be creative. They stimulate critical thinking and encourage others to collaborate with them toward shared goals. They have the ability to develop leadership capacity in others (Atwater & Wright, 1996; Lynch, 2012) and engage in mentoring others to help them develop leadership knowledge and skills, take initiative and accept responsibility (Bass & Riggio, 2006). Transformational leaders evaluate the situations in which they lead and draw on a range of leadership strategies appropriate to address ongoing change. They define the reasons change is necessary and as a result, when organisational change may occur organisational members are more satisfied and group cohesiveness improves.

4   Servant Leadership

Similarly to the transformational leadership perspective, servant leadership is also people oriented. Both types of leadership involve elements of integrity, trust, respect, delegation, vision, and influence on followers. Both perspectives also advocate mentoring, recognition, listening skills, empowering followers, empathy, foresight, stewardship, commitment to growth of others and building a trusting community through which organizational goals can be met (Lynch, 2012; Spears, 1996). However, servant leadership differs in that the servant leader's focus shifts from his or her own interests to the development of the people he or she serves (Greenleaf, 1970, 2003; Lynch, 2012). The collective welfare of the followers is equally important to the organisational goals and the process is more important than the end result. Spears (2010) condensed Greenleaf's writings into the following ten characteristics of the servant leader:

1   Listening receptively to what is being said and unsaid and being in touch with one's inner voice.
2   Striving to understand and empathize with others.
3   Healing relationships.
4   Strengthening awareness: of self and others to better understand values, ethics and issues of power.
5   Persuading rather than coercing.

6 Balancing conceptual thinking and operational realities.
7 Having foresight to understand the past, present and the likely consequences of the future.
8 Serving the needs of others.
9 Committing to the growth of self and others.
10 Building community.

Servant leadership also addresses the spiritual element of a person's life and the human need for meaning (Kibby & Hartel, 2004). Instead of one compelling vision articulated by the transformational leader, a servant leader acknowledges multiple visions and diverse cultural meanings (Sackney, Walker, & Mitchell, 1999).

5   Shared Leadership

Recent leadership literature has also distinguished between leading as the quality of one person and leadership as a collective phenomenon referred to as shared, collective or distributed leadership (Harris, 2005; Spillane, 2006). Leadership from this perspective is seen as a process centered on the interdependent relationships across the organisation rather than on individuals (Spillane, 2006). Shared leadership is seen as the professional work of everyone (Lambert, 2002) and is no longer bounded by formal title or position.

Sophisticated knowledge work calls for self management and the development of leadership in every member of an organization (Spillane, 2006). From this perspective, individuals are empowered to take action making their work more meaningful and effective. In the context of education, this takes the form of shared responsibilities among school leaders, teachers and parents. Rather than focusing on leadership behaviors, shared leadership is the result of social relationships leading to responsibility, learning, mutual respect, sharing (Gastil, 1997) and a greater capacity for school improvement. It empowers and grants greater autonomy for teaching, learning, creativity and innovation.

According to Nemerowicz and Rosi (1997) shared leadership has the following characteristics: a common good is sought; democratic processes, honesty and shared ethics are highly valued; people are interdependent and all are active participants in the process of leadership; each person works to enhance the process and to make it more fulfilling and the quality of people's interactions is the distinguishing factor rather than their position.

For Lawler (2001) a shared leadership approach can vary dependent upon who is included and the balance those included actually have between autonomy and control. It can occur when organizations replace hierarchical structures with lateral forms of organization that rely on teams, networks, technology, agile structures, and employee participation. However, hierarchies do not necessarily preclude shared leadership which can still operate within hierarchical organizations in the form of teams, committees, informal work groups (Harris, 2005; Harris & Chapman, 2002) and communities of practice (Wenger, 1998; Wenger-Treyner et al., 2014).

Many of the characteristics of shared leadership are evident in the concept of teacher leadership also prevalent in the wider leadership literature and another critical component to understanding leadership in the educational context. Typically teacher leader roles have been at three levels – the classroom, the organization and profession (Kurtz, 2009). Teacher leadership is anchored in the belief that all individuals have knowledge and skills that can be shared to enhance individual and collective learning in a school (Stephenson, 2011; Stephenson, Dada, & Harold, 2012) and that "no one has a monopoly of knowledge and thus all stakeholders in the school should come together to bring about real sustainable change" (Lynch, 2012, p. 183).

6   Positive Leadership

Similarly to shared leadership (Harris, 2005; Spillane, 2006), positive leadership (Cameron, 2008) advocate for a systems approach based on the belief that educational organisations are networks of relationships rather than mere collections of individuals (Buller, 2015).

Positive leadership fosters resilience through positive relationships and experiences. It also is dependent on positive climate, positive communication and positive meaning (Cameron, 2008; Cameron, Dutton, & Quinn, 2003).

> Positive leadership builds on a combination of stable traits, malleable states, and situational factors ... These traits, processes, behaviors and performance outcomes are manifested at various levels, including leaders, their followers and their organizations. (Youssef-Morgan & Luthans, 2013, p. 201)

The above characteristics of positive educational leadership are consistent with dimensions of leadership in the literature. However, what is unique to positive leadership is that its focus is on strengths and capabilities and on affirming developmental potential (Cameron, 2008; Youssef-Morgan & Luthans, 2012, 2013). "Its orientation is toward enabling thriving and flourishing rather than toward addressing obstacles and impediments" (Cameron, 2008, p. 2).

For Buller (2015) we can recognize positive leadership when there is a greater emphasis on developing what is already working than on correcting what is flawed. Positive leadership encourages leaders to spend more time with their best performers; personalizes and differentiates the subtle guidance given rather than assuming that a single leadership style works best for all people; adopts a systems approach, emphasizing group and unique contributions of each member and treats each member as a capable member; explores what is possible instead of being bound by past decisions and disappointments; emphasizes rewards and recognitions over punishments and penalties; is both people and goal-oriented; and prefers team-based and collaborative approaches (pp. 10–16).

With its focus on developmental potential, positive leadership encourages professional and personal learning and growth of self and others. The concept of leaders as learners and the importance of valuing learning for all educational leaders is affirmed by scholars such as Dinham (2016); Hattie (2012, 2013), Hattie and Yates (2014); Roberston and Timplerly (2011); Robinson (2011), Sharratt and Planche (2016), and Timperley (2011).

7   Leading Learning and Teaching

The concept of leading learning and teaching has re-emerged in the educational leadership literature recently and it draws upon the leadership literature that has preceded it including past and current broader leadership theory and practice (Bush, 2011). Educational leaders can no longer only focus on the organisational functions of schools and educational systems but must also be instructional leaders placing student learning as the first priority (Du Plessis, 2013). As such the emphasis on leading learning and teaching is placed at the centre of educational leadership and leadership development rather than a focus on the art and science of leadership. It advocates foregrounding up to date knowledge of learning in order to improve equity and current practice. That is, knowledge of learning and teaching is integrated into, rather than separated from the work of school, organisation and systems where leaders attempt to influence teaching, coaching and mentoring practices that improve intended learning outcomes (Dinham, 2016; Robinson, 2016).

Teaching and learning are social enactments, and educational leaders are accountable for the development of an effective learning and teaching space (Jordan, Kleinsasser, & Roe, 2014) and teachers' improved learning and teaching practices (Fink, Markholt, & Bransford, 2011; Kemmis et al., 2014; Robinson, 2011). Recent research in leading learning and teaching reminds us of the importance of vision; establishing goals and expectations; promoting and participating in professional learning and development; planning, coordinating and evaluating teaching, learning and the curriculum, resourcing strategically and ensuring a safe, orderly and supportive environment (Dinham, 2016; Robinson, Hohepa, & Lloyd, 2009; Robinson, 2007). However, leading learning and teaching is complex, contested, nuanced, fluid and situated in context. The choice of instructional leadership strategies determine the amount of time leaders spend on critical reflection and incidental interaction with staff members. Educational leaders who spend a significant amount of time in their offices become disconnected from what is actually happening within classrooms (Spillane, Camburn, & Pareja, 2007). Therefore, educational leaders need to focus on the teachers in classrooms before they can expect positive changes in schools and education systems (Du Pleissis, 2013).

Robinson et al.'s (2009) Best Evidence Synthesis identifies the dimensions of leading learning and teaching that have the most impact on student learning. These are:

1 Establishing Goals and Expectations: Includes the setting, communicating and monitoring of learning goals, standards and expectations, and the involvement of staff and others in the process so that there is clarity and consensus about goals.
2 Strategic Resourcing: Involves aligning resource selection and allocation to priority teaching goals. Includes provision of appropriate expertise through staff recruitment
3 Planning, Coordinating and Evaluating Teaching and the Curriculum: Direct involvement in the support and evaluation of teaching through regular classroom visits and provision of formative and summative feedback to teachers. Direct oversight of curriculum through school-wide coordination across classes and year levels and alignment to school goals.
4 Promoting and Participating in Teacher Learning and Development: Leadership that not only promotes but directly participates with teachers in formal or informal professional learning and
5 Ensuring an Orderly and Supportive Environment: Protecting time for teaching and learning by reducing external pressures and interruptions and establishing an orderly and supportive environment both inside and outside classrooms (Robinson, 2007, p. 12).

Robinson (2007) highlights for educational leaders the importance of creating the conditions to enable educational leaders to do this important leading learning work and of influencing teaching practices that matter. "There is much to be gained from a closer integration of leadership theory and research with demonstrably effective pedagogical practices and teacher learning" (Robinson, 2007, p. 15).

8   Educational Leadership from an Islamic Perspective

Shah (2006, 2010) reminds us that different societies and cultures have varying interpretations of educational leadership reflecting their specific values, beliefs and practices. As such it is critical to consider educational leadership in the UAE from a cultural and Islamic perspective.

Knowledge and learning are given great importance in Islam. The Quran and hadith are considered to be the foundation of all knowledge and seeking and acquiring knowledge is a duty imposed by Allah. As such, in Islam, educational leaders are seen as role models, teachers and mentors who should be constant seekers and givers of knowledge. Shah (2006) describes a three-dimensional model of leadership involving teaching with knowledge and understanding, guiding with wisdom and values; and caring with responsibility and commitment.

Islamic notions of leadership share several important perspectives also found in Western literature. For example, just as in Schon's (1983) theory of reflective leadership practice, reflection and meditation are highly emphasized in Islamic theory and practice. The challenge for today's leaders is 'how,' 'when' and to 'what extent' reflection and action can be balanced (Shah, 2006). Other similarities include concepts such as values, morality, collaboration and sharing and consultative decision making. Bolman and Deal (2002) suggest that leaders need to go beyond the capacities of their heads and listen with their hearts and talk of leading with soul. Leadership is understood then as cognitive, emotional, and spiritual. Such concepts can be found particularly in transformational, distributed and servant leadership (Shah, 2006, 2010). According to Sarayrah (2004), servant leadership is deeply rooted in Arab/Islamic culture with many similarities between servant leadership and pre-Islamic and early Islamic leadership styles and practices. The Arab preIslamic value system emphasised personal characteristics of courage, mercy, generosity, equality, power, honesty, humility, patience and forgiveness (Sarayrah, 2004). However, with the introduction of Islam some of the existing kin based Bedouin values at that time were duly moderated to better promote equity and social justice.

Recent western leadership literature invariably challenges the evolving triad of identifying a common purpose or vision, seeking opportunities and building relationships and rather advocates for a transpersonal approach that acknowledges that all people have value. Transpersonal leadership (Knights, 2011) recognizes the importance of self awareness, understanding one's mental models and mindsets, as these impact leadership behaviours. This can only be achieved by the leader raising their level of consciousness so that a true understanding of their values is used in every decision made (Knights, 2017, p. 9). The focus is also on actualizing relationships of emergent potential. With its emphasis on care, self potential and the potentials of others transpersonal leadership can be realized through relationships, ethical behaviours and authenticity. According to Knights (2017) to be an ethical leader it is necessary to develop personal conscience values such as fairness and forgiveness as well as self determination values such as purpose, courage and resilience (Wall & Knights, 2013). Developing such leadership capacity is therefore necessarily iterative, organic, holistic and requires considerable time and effort.

Whilst Knights (2011) analyzes leadership in the business world much of what he discusses is applicable to the educational context. His definition of transpersonal leadership draws on several other leadership perspectives including servant/service and stewardship, inspiration and vision, self knowledge and facilitation of the learning of others. The transpersonal leader is characterized as someone who 'thinks beyond his/her ego' is emotionally intelligent, ethical and authentic (Knights, 2011). The notion of 'stewardship' means that leaders "weigh not only their own needs and desires and those of stakeholders but also those of future generations" (p. 35). Knights' definition resonates with many of the values related to Islamic perspectives on leadership as identified by Shah (2006).

Wheatley (1992) reminds us that leadership is context dependent and the context is established by the relationships we value. Relational leadership then is a view of leadership and organization "as human social constructions that emanate from the rich connections and interdependencies of organizations and their members" (Uhl Bien, 2006, p. 655). Leadership then is regarded as an interactive process of collaboration that occurs between leaders and followers where authority and influence are shared (Rost, 1991). Relational leadership practices can also be classified as transpersonal (Knights, 2011).

For Komives, Lucas, and McMahon (2013) relational leadership is inclusive, empowering, purposeful, ethical, and process oriented. For leaders to be regarded as ethical leaders they must be attractive and credible role models (Brown & Trevino, 2006). Demonstrating care and concern and treating others fairly attracts followers as does credibility. Ethical leaders are credible because they are trustworthy and model ethical behaviours.

An 'authentic' approach emphasizes consistency between the leader's moral and ethical values and their practices (see Avolio & Gardner, 2005; Begley, 2006; Hodgkinson, 1991, 1996; Sergiovanni, 1992). For Bhindhi, Smith, and Hansen (n.d., p. 3) authentic leadership is "the transformation of oneself and others to a higher moral and ethical purpose. It is earned by the leader and bestowed by followers." Authentic leadership then is dependent upon the recognized integrity and credibility of the leader (Duignan & Bhindi, 1997). It is a dynamic and collective process which recognizes the critical relationship between leader and follower. It results in both greater self awareness and self regulated positive behaviors on the part of leaders.

> Authenticity is knowing, and acting on, what is true and real inside yourself, your team and your organization and knowing and acting on what is true and real in the world. It is not enough to walk one's talk if one is headed off, or leading one's organization, community or nation, off a cliff! (Terry, n.d.)

Authentic leadership fosters positive self development and encompasses a positive moral perspective (Duignan & Bhindi, 1997; Begley, 2006; Luthans & Avolio, 2003; May et al., 2003). For Avolio and Gardner (2005) authentic leaders have a deep sense of self and a conscious commitment to core, enduring beliefs, principles, values and ethics modeled in all that they do. This earns them the trust of others. Authentic leaders' confidence, hope and optimism stems from their strong beliefs in themselves (Luthans & Youssef, 2004). They make clear to others exactly what is expected at individual, dyad, group and organizational levels. As such, authentic followers display behavior paralleling what characterizes authentic leaders such as internalized regulatory processes, balanced processing of information, and relational transparency (Avolio & Gardner, 2005). Through authentic leadership people are better able to find meaning and connection at work through greater self awareness. Optimism, confidence, hope, mutual trust, commitment and resiliency are also restored by promoting positive ethical climates, transparent relationships, and inclusive structures and decision making (Avolio & Gardner, 2005).

In Islam values such as integrity, caring, justice and the distinction between right and wrong are also emphasized and self discipline and character building expected. For Islamic leadership then, the source of these values is derived from faith and religious philosophy (Sarayrah, 2004).

According to Shah (2006), the Islamic advocacy of equality, fraternity, collaboration and sharing can be found in the form of shared leadership which favors democratic practices and effective communication. Such an approach when grounded within an Islamic perspective necessarily engages many people in leadership activity where the focus is holistic learner development (Shah, 2006, 2010). This in turn aligns with the transformational leadership perspective "providing both intellectual stimulation and individual support to all those being led" (Shah, 2006, p. 377).

A further leadership perspective is evident in the dialogical (consultative) Al Shura leadership model which reflects the region's own culture and traditions, and in turn informs the style of leadership in schools (Al Hinai & Rutherford, 2002). The Shura principle, deeply rooted in Islam, is defined as the process of extensive discussion of an issue from all its aspects and dimensions, selection of the best given views on that issue, and testing of those views to make sure that the best interests of the community are realized (Abul-Faris, 1980).

There is a burgeoning literature on female leadership in general (see Kemp, Madsen, & El-Saidi, 2013) and educational leadership in particular (see Al Nuaimi et al., 2015; Bond, 2013; Samier, 2015; Thorne, 2011; Zahran et al., 2016) emerging from recent studies and commentary within the UAE itself. Much of this is centered on the impact of globalization and educational policy borrowing on leadership development. This reflects the UAE government's push to make the Emirates internationally competitive in the 21st century. Zahran et al. (2016), for example, note that the Global Education Network has emphasized 'universal' values including tolerance, solidarity, equality, justice, inclusion, cooperation and non-violence as underpinning a global education perspective. Such values appear to overlap with the Islamic perspectives outlined by Shah (2006) and yet Abdelkarim and Hann (2002, cited in Zahran et al., 2016) remind us that 'best practices' from one system may not necessarily be congruent with the social, cultural and religious perspectives in another. Macpherson, Kachelhoffer, and Elnemr (2007) support this point with their emphasis on leading learning and teaching. Their view is that to meet the needs of UAE educational restructuring an 'educative, indigenized leadership' was required with school leaders who would implement school reform "through collaborative work planning, participative budgeting, promoting interactive pedagogy, developing extra-curricular activities, evaluation and community communication, and engaging parent and other community representatives in governance" (p. 8).

In Bond's (2013) study of four female Emirati vice principals, her participants commented on the gap that was apparent between the Western content

of their teacher and educational leader preparation and the expectations
of parents and the community when it came to cultural and social norms.
These school leaders wanted a greater focus on Emirati perspectives in
their training including strategies for communicating with the families and
handling conflict. Thorne (2011) also noted the tension between external
policy borrowing and the internal UAE context stating that "in essence the
country seems to be looking for the 'magic bullet' from outside rather than
favoring a homegrown, more organic solution to the problems" (p. 174). The
impact of Western teachers and educational advisers was noted by students
in Dickson's (2013) study who had experienced the changes in teaching and
curriculum. They expressed concerns that the emphasis on English language
was undermining their Arabic language, the language of their religion, and
that some students were copying aspects of Western culture that may be
in conflict with local cultural expectations. What is apparent in the more
recent literature related to the UAE is a tension between the globalization of
educational restructuring practices and their impact on local Islamic cultural
norms.

9   Gender and Leadership

During the final quarter of the 20th century much attention was focused on
the issue of gender and leadership, in both Western and Islamic contexts, driven
predominantly by feminist research agendas which aimed to understand the
nature of women's leadership practices and also to explain gender-related
inequalities in leadership positions. Appelbaum, Audet, and Miller (2003)
identify four schools of thought that had developed; biology and sex, gender
roles, environmental factors and attitudinal drivers. They conclude that a
redirection of research is needed, which, rather than focusing on differences
between the genders, needs to link to "the individual, rather than to an
individual's sex or even gender role" (p. 49). Van Engen and Willemsen (2004)
suggests that there are still remnants of sex differences in leadership styles but
that these may be more affected by culturally embedded perceptions rather
than gender per se. As we do, they believe leadership is a highly contextualized
phenomenon and their results need to be considered closely in relation to
the study, and perceptual and organizational factors. What has resulted from
two-dimensional, dichotomous models (e.g. task versus personal orientation,
democratic versus autocratic styles) underpinning research is further confusion
and contradictory findings. Van Engen and Willemsen (2004) suggest that
the reality of leadership is far more complex. Sex differences in leadership

style attributed to women may be more related to the fact that women tend to work with and lead other women, and often lead in 'stereotypical' female contexts. The participants in this book worked mainly in female predominant contexts, (although two went on to more traditionally male oriented fields including business and politics). Although there is currently a surge of interest in research in the Middle East in the field of women's achievements including leadership, it is equally important to frame research questions and findings in terms of context. Therefore, gender is less critical than style and strategy and their impact on those led.

10   Conclusion

This chapter briefly describes situational, transformational, servant, shared and positive leadership perspectives. It also addresses leading learning and teaching and leadership from an Islamic perspective. These perspectives were chosen because they resonate best with the leadership practices of the five Dubai women. They all focus on the importance of networks and relationships. Apart from the shared leadership perspective they all also include authenticity and a moral/ethical component typically found in authentic, ethical and transpersonal leadership perspectives (Avolio & Gardner, 2005; Luthans & Avolio, 2003; May, Chan, Hodges, & Avolio, 2003; Knights, 2011, 2017). Similarly to Shah (2006, 2010) the authors argue that educational leaders and researchers in the Gulf region have a responsibility to enhance learning and teaching and to develop a knowledge base that is respectful and more inclusive of Islamic perspectives and that can improve mutual understanding in support of the common good and a more pluralistic society.

In the following chapters of this book we explore the leadership beliefs, perspectives and practices of five Emirati educational leaders using a narrative inquiry approach and taking this multidimensional leadership perspective.

References

Abul-Faris, A. (1980). *The political system of Islam.* Amman: The Library of the Modern Message.

Al Hinai, H., & Rutherford, D. (2002, September 20–22). *Exploring the Alshura school leadership model in Oman.* Paper presented at the Annual Conference of the British Educational Leadership, Management and Administration Society (BELMAS), Birmingham, England.

Al Nuaimi, S., Chowdhury, H., Eleftheriou, K., & Katsioloudes, M. I. (2015). Participative decision-making and job satisfaction for teachers in the UAE. *International Journal of Educational Management, 29*(5), 645–665. http://doi.org/10.1108/IJEM-07-2014-0090

Allix, N. M. (2000). Transformational leadership: Democratic or despotic? *Educational Management and Administration, 28*(1), 7–20.

Appelbaum, S. H., Audet, L., & Miller, J. C. (2003). Gender and leadership? Leadership and gender? A journey through the landscape of theories. *Leadership & Organization Development Journal, 24*(1), 43–51.

Atwater, L., & Wright, W. (1996). Power and transformational and transactional leadership in public and private organizations. *International Journal of Public Administration, 19*(6), 963–998.

Avolio, B. J., & Gardner, W. L. (2005). Authentic leadership development: Getting to the root of positive forms of leadership. *The Leadership Quarterly, 16*, 315–338.

Bass, B. M. (1997). *The ethics of transformational leadership* (Kellogg Leadership Studies Project, Transformational Leadership Working Papers). College Park, MD: The James MacGregor Burns Academy of Leadership Press.

Bass, B. M. (1990). From transactional to transformational leadership: Learning to share the vision. *Organizational Dynamics, 18*(3), 19–31.

Bass, B. M., & Avolio, B. J. (Eds.). (1994). *Improving organizational effectiveness through transformational leadership*. Thousand Oaks, CA: Sage Publications.

Bass, B. M., & Riggio, J. (2006). *Transformational leadership* (2nd ed.). New York, NY: Free Press.

Begley, P. T. (2006). Self-knowledge, capacity and sensitivity: Prerequisites to authentic leadership by school principals. *Journal of Educational Administration, 44*(6), 570–589.

Bhindi, N., Smith, R., Hansen, J., & Riley, D. (n.d.). *Authentic leadership in education: A cross-country phenomenon – or, leaders in their own mind?* Retrieved from http://www.woodhillpark.com/attachments/1/NZEALS%20%20Authentic%20 Leadership%20Summary.pdf

Bolman, L.G., & Deal, T.E. (2002). Leading with soul and spirit. *School Administrator, 59*(2), 21–26.

Bond, S. (2013). *Educational development in the context of the United Arab Emirates: Participant perceptions of the XXXX professional development program* (Unpublished doctoral dissertation). University of Florida, Gainesville, FL. Retrieved from https://search.proquest.com/docview/1564044873?pq-origsite=gscholar

Bourdieu, P. (1984). *Distinction: A social critique of the judgement of taste* (R. Nice, Trans.). Cambridge, MA: Harvard University Press.

Brown, M. E., & Treviño, L. K. (2006). Ethical leadership: A review and future directions. *Leadership Quarterly, 17*, 595–616.

Buller, J. L. (2015). *Positive academic leadership: How to stop putting out fires and start making a difference*. San Francisco, CA: Jossey-Bass.

Burns, J. M. (1978). *Leadership*. New York, NY: Harper & Row.

Bush, T. (2003).Theory and practice in educational management. In T. Bush, M. Coleman, & M. Thurlow (Eds.), *Leadership and strategic management in South African schools*. London: Commonwealth Secretariat.

Bush, T. (2011). *Theories of educational leadership and management* (4th ed.). London: Sage Publications.

Bush, T., & Glover, D. (2014). School leadership models: What do we know. *School Leadership and Management, 34*(5), 553–571. doi:10.1080/13632434.2014.928680

Cameron, K. S. (2008). *Positive leadership: Strategies for extraordinary performance*. San Francisco, CA: Berrett-Koehler Publishers.

Cameron, K. S., Dutton, J. E., & Quinn, R. E. (Eds.). (2003). *Positive organisational scholarship*. San Francisco, CA: Berrett-Koehler Publishers.

Carew, D. K., Parisi-Carew, E., & Blanchard, K. H. (1986). Group development and situational leadership: A model for managing groups. *Training & Development Journal, 40*(6), 46–50.

Conger, J. A. (1990). The dark side of leadership. *Organizational Dynamics, 19*(2), 44–45.

Dickson, M. (2013). School improvements in Abu Dhabi, United Arab Emirates: Asking the expert witnesses. *Improving Schools 16*(3), 272–284.

Dimmock, C. (2000). *Designing the learning-centred school: A cross cultural perspective* (pp. 33–44). London: Falmer Press.

Dimmock, C. (2002). Cross-cultural differences in interpreting and doing research. In M. Coleman & A. R. J. Briggs (Eds.), *Research methods in educational leadership and management* (pp. 28–42). London: Sage Publications.

Dinham, S. (2016). *Leading learning and teaching*. Camberwell: ACER Press.

Duignan, P., & Bhindi, N. (1997). Authenticity in leadership: An emerging perspective. *Journal of Educational Administration, 35*(3), 195–209.

Du Plessis, P. (2013). The principal as instructional leader: Guiding schools to improve instruction. *Education as Change, 17*(1), 79–92.

Fink, S., Markholt, A., & Bransford, J. (2011). *Leading for instructional improvement: How successful leaders develop teaching and learning expertise*. San Francisco, CA: Jossey-Bass.

Gastil, J. (1997). A definition and illustration of democratic leadership. In K. Grint (Ed.), *Leadership*. Oxford: Oxford University Press.

Gill, R. (2006). *Theory and practice of leadership*. Thousand Oaks, CA: Sage Publications.

Greenleaf, R. K. (1970). *The servant as leader* (pp. 1–37). Indianapolis, IN: The Robert K. Greenleaf Center.

Greenleaf, R. K. (1977). *Servant leadership: A journey into the nature of legitimate power and greatness*. New York, NY: Paulist Press.

Greenleaf, R. K. (2003). *The servant-leader within: A transformative path*. New York, NY: Paulist Press.

Harris, A. (2005). Distributed leadership. In B. Davies (Ed.), *The essentials of school leadership*. London: Paul Chapman.

Harris, A., & Chapman, C. (2002). *Democratic leadership for school improvement in challenging contexts*. Paper presented at International Congress on School Effectiveness and Improvement, Copenhagen.

Hattie, J. (2012). *Visible learning for teachers: Maximizing impact on achievement*. Oxford: Routledge.

Hattie, J. (2013). *Understanding learning: Lessons for learning, teaching and research*. Presentation at ACER Research Conference 2013. http://dx.doi.org/10.1016/j.colegn.2017.03.00

Hattie, J., & Yates, G. (2014). *Visible learning and the science of how we learn*. Oxford: Routledge.

Hersey, P. (1985). *The situational leader*. New York, NY: Warner Books.

Hersey, P., & Blanchard, K. H. (1993). *Management of organizational behavior: Utilizing human resources*. Englewood Cliffs, NJ: Prentice Hall.

Hodgkinson, C. (1991). *Educational leadership: The moral art*. Albany, NY: State University of New York Press.

Hodgkinson, C. (1996). *Administrative philosophy*. Oxford: Elsevier-Pergamon.

Jordan, M. E., Kleinsasser, R. C., & Roe, M. F. (2014). Wicked problems: Inescapable wickedity. *Journal of Education for Teaching: International Research and Pedagogy, 40*(4), 415–430.

Kemmis, S., Wilkinson, J., Edwards-Groves, C., Hardy, I., Grootenboer, P., & Bristol, L. (2014). *Changing practices, changing education*. Singapore: Springer Press.

Kemp, L. J., Madsen, S. R., & El-Saidi, M. (2013). The current state of female educational leadership in the United Arab Emirates. *Journal of Global Responsibility, 4*(1) 99–112.

Kibby, L & Hartel, C. (2004). Skills that enact the behaviors of servant-leadership. *Gallup Leadership Institute Summit*, 1–10.

Knights, J. (2011). *The invisible elephant & the pyramid treasure*. London: Tomorrows Company. Retrieved from http://www.leadershape.biz/invisible-elephant

Knights, J. (2017). *Ethical leadership: How to develop ethical leaders* (White Paper). Retrieved June 01, 2017, from https://www.routledge.com/posts/9951

Komives, S. R., Lucas, N., & McMahon, T. R. (2013). *Exploring leadership: For college students who want to make a difference* (3rd ed.). San Francisco, CA: Jossey-Bass.

Kurtz, S. (2009). Teacher leadership. *Leadership, 39*(1), 12–14.

Lambert, L. (2002). *Leadership capacity for lasting school improvement*. Alexandria, VA: Association for Supervision and Curriculum Development.

Lawler, E. E. (2001). The era of human capital has finally arrived. In W. Bennis, G. M. Spreitzer, & T. G. Cummings (Eds.), *The future of leadership* (pp. 14–25). San Francisco, CA: Jossey Bass.

Luthans, F., & Avolio, B. J. (2003). Authentic leadership: A positive developmental approach. In K. S. Cameron, J. E. Dutton, & R. E. Quinn (Eds.), *Positive organizational scholarship* (pp. 241–261). San Francisco, CA: Barrett-Koehler.

Luthans, F., & Youssef, C. M. (2004). Human, social, and now positive psychological capital management: Investing in people for competitive advantage. *Organizational Dynamics, 33*(2), 143–160.

Lynch, M. (2012). *A guide to effective school leadership theories.* New York, NY: Rouledge.

Macpherson, R., Kachelhoffer, P., & El Nemr, M. (2007). The radical modernization of school and education system leadership in the United Arab Emirates: Towards indigenized and educative leadership. *International Studies in Educational Administration, 35*(1), 60–77.

May, D. R., Chan, A. Y. I., Hodges, T. D., & Avolio, B. J. (2003). Developing the moral component of authentic leadership. *Organizational Dynamics, 33*(3), 247–260.

Morrison, E. W. (1994). Role definitions and organizational citizenship behaviour: The importance of the employees' perspective. *Academy of Management Journal, 37,* 1543–1567.

Nemerowicz, G., & Rosi, E. (1997). *Education for leadership and social responsibility.* London: Falmer.

Northouse, P. (2007). *Leadership: Theory and practice.* Thousand Oaks, CA: Sage Publications.

Robertson, J., & Timperley, S. (Eds.). (2011). *Leadership and learning.* London: Sage Publications.

Robinson, V. (2007). *The impact of leadership on student outcomes: Making sense of the evidence.* Retrieved from http://research.acer.edu.au/research_conference_2007/5

Robinson, V. (2011). *Student-centred leadership.* San Francisco, CA: Jossey-Bass.

Robinson, V. (2016). Foreword. In S. Dinham (Ed.), *Leading learning and teaching.* Camberwell: ACER Press.

Robinson, V., Hohepa, C., & Lloyd, M. (2009). *School leadership and student outcomes: Identifying what works and why: Best Evidence Synthesis Iteration (BES).* Wellington: Crown. Retrieved from http://www.educationcounts.govt.nz/__data/assets/pdf_file/0015/60180/BESLeadership-Web.pdf

Rost, J. C. (1991). *Leadership for the twenty-first century.* Westport, CT: Praeger.

Sackney, L., Walker, K., & Mitchell, C. (1999). Postmodern conceptions of power for educational leadership. *Journal of Educational Administration and Foundations, 14*(1), 33–57.

Samier, E. (2015). Emirati women's higher educational leadership formation under globalization: Culture, religion, politics and the dialectics of modern civilization. *Gender and Education, 27*(3), 239–254. http://dx.doi.org/10.1080/09540253.2015.1028901

Sarayrah, Y. K. (2004). Servant leadership in the Bedouin-Arab culture. *Global Virtual Ethics Review, 5*(3), 58–79.

Schon, D. (1983). *The reflective practitioner: How professionals think in action.* New York, NY: Basic Books.

Sergiovanni, T. (1992). *Moral leadership.* San Francisco, CA: Jossey-Bass Inc.

Shah, S. (2006). Educational leadership: An Islamic perspective. *British Educational Research Journal, 32*(3), 363–385.

Shah, S. (2010). Educational leadership: An Islamic perspective. In T. Abbas (Ed.), *Islam and education* (pp. 141–166). London: Routledge.

Shah, S. (2016). *Education, leadership and Islam: Theories, discourses and practices from an Islamic perspective.* London & New York, NY: Routledge, Taylor & Francis Group.

Sharratt, L., & Planche, B. (2016). *Leading collaborative learning: Empowering excellence.* Thousand Oaks, CA: Corwin.

Spears, L. (1996). Reflections on Robert K. Greenleaf and servant-leadership. *Leadership & Organization Development Journal, 17*, 33–35.

Spears, L. (2010). Character and servant leadership: Ten characteristics of efffective, caring leaders. *The Journal of Virtues & Leadership, 1*(1), 25–30.

Spillane, J. P. (2006). *Distributed leadership.* San Francisco, CA: Jossey-Bass.

Spillane, J. P., Camburn, E. M., & Pareja, A. S. (2007). Taking a distributed perspective to the school principal's workday. *Leadership and Policy in Schools, 6*(1), 103–125. doi:10.1080/15700760601091200

Starrat, R. (2001). Democratic leadership theory in late modernity: An oxymoron or ironic possibility? *International Journal of Leadership in Education, 4*(4), 333–352.

Stephenson, L. (2011). *Conducting an investigation into the nature of teacher leadership and its impact on school improvement.* Abu Dhabi: Abu Dhabi Education Council-Research Office.

Stephenson, L., Dada, R., & Harold, B. (2012). Challenging the traditional idea of leadership in UAE schools. *On the Horizon, 20*(1), 54–63. https://doi.org/10.1108/10748121211202071

Terry, R. (n.d.). *Authentic leadership: Courage in action.* Retrieved November 10, 2010, from http://www.action-wheel.com/authentic-leadership.html

Thorne, C. (2011). The impact of educational reforms on the work of the school principal in the United Arab Emirates. *Educational Management, Administration and Leadership, 39*(2), 172–185. doi:10.1177/1741143210390058

Timperley, H. S. (2011). Knowledge and the leadership of learning. *Leadership and Policy in Schools, 10*(2), 145–170.

Uhl Bien, M. (2006). Relational leadership theory: Exploring the social processes of leadership and organizing. *The Leadership Quarterly, 17*(6), 654–676.

Van Engen, M. L., & Willemsen, T. L. (2004). Sex and leadership styles: A meta-analysis of research published in the 1990s. *Psychological Reports, 94*(1), 3–18.

Wall, T., & Knights, J. (2013). *Leadership assessment for talent development*. London: Kogan Page.

Wenger, E. (1998). *Communities of practice: Learning, meaning, and identity.* Cambridge: Cambridge University Press.

Wenger-Trayner, E., Fenton-O'Creevy, M., Hutchinson, S., Kubiak, C., & Wenger-Trayner, B. (Eds.). (2014). *Learning in landscapes of practice*. London: Routledge.

Wheatley, M. J. (1992). *Leadership and the new science: Learning about organization from an orderly universe*. San Francisco, CA: Berrett-Kohler Publishers.

Wofford, J. C., Whittington, J. L., & Goodwin, V. L. (2001). Follower motive patterns as situational moderators for transformational leadership effectiveness. *Journal of Managerial Issues, 13*, 196–211.

Youssef-Morgan, C. M., & Luthans, F. (2012). Positive global leadership. *Journal of World Business, 27*, 539–547.

Youssef-Morgan, C. M., & Luthans, F. (2013). *Positive leadership: Meaning and application across cultures* (Paper 127). Lincoln, NE: Management Department Faculty Publications. Retrieved from http://digitalcommons.unl.edu/managementfacpub/127

Zahran, R., Pettaway, L. D., Waller, L., & Waller, S. (2016). Educational leadership: Challenges in the United Arab Emirates. *The Global eLearning Journal, 5*(1), 1–8.

CHAPTER 4

Raya Rashid (Um Dalmook)

My mother rules my life. She is always there guiding, supporting and encouraging me.

∴

Raya's legacy is her selfless approach to her family and community, constantly finding time to share her wisdom and knowledge about Islam and life for the benefit of others.

Raya Rashid (Um Dalmook) is a well-respected citizen of Shandagha in Dubai, widely known as mutawa'a Um Dalmook, who has contributed in many significant ways to her family and community. She was educated as a young woman at a time when most girls received minimal education and was recognized early as a leader with the capacity to take on the role of 'mutawa'a' to teach the Holy Quran to children in her community. As a mother and grandmother she is a life-long learner who has always searched for ways to deepen her understanding of Islam and to promote its values among family and society.

1   Raya's Story

On a sunny mid-morning in November 1963 a group of young children – 5 girls and 6 boys – left their homes and moved towards a small areesh near the beach in Dubai. The boys ran towards the areesh calling out to each other as they converged while the girls walked more quietly in a small group accompanied by a young woman, mother to two of them. As they neared the building they all became more serious. The young mutawa'a (teacher), named Raya, greeted each of them with a smile as they came quietly into the room. One of the boys approached Raya shyly with a basket of sweet cakes.

"My mother sent these for you, mutawa'a," he said.

The children sat cross-legged on a woven mat on the floor, boys on one side, girls on the other. Each child opened their copy of the Holy Qu'ran on a small wooden mirfaa in front of them. Raya chatted with them for a few minutes as they settled, reminding them of what had been shared the previous day. She

© KONINKLIJKE BRILL NV, LEIDEN, 2018 | DOI 10.1163/9789004372948_004

began reading from the Holy Qu'ran then paused and asked the children to repeat the passage. Their clear voices sounded out the special words in unison. Raya smiled and praised them for their effort.

"Now let me hear you say this hadith one at a time" she said. "Ahmed, can you begin please ...."

The other children listened attentively as Raya guided the young boy through the words.

"Now, Mouza, can you do as well as Ahmed? Let me hear you."

One by one the children repeated the particular hadith. Outside the areesh Raya's mother paused listening to her daughter with a satisfied smile.

"How right I was to encourage her to become a mutawa'a," she thought to herself. "She has such deep knowledge of the Holy Qu'ran and the children's parents have such respect for her and what she is doing for these young ones."

Thirty years later three generations of Emirati women were gathered at the Heritage Village[1] in Shindagha.

Raya's abaya and shayla rustled softly in the wind as she gazed out across the sea, dreaming a little. Her daughter's voice brought her back to reality. Maryam was talking to her aunt and uncle, visiting from Abu Dhabi, as they strolled through the Village in Shindagha.

"Things have changed quite a bit since we lived here as children" she was saying. "Dubai has grown so fast and become so modern. In some ways things were simpler in the past but in many ways they were not easy." Maryam turned, smiling, to her mother.

"Umi, you remember from when I was little and you were teaching the children in our house." Raya smiled in response.

"Of course habibti, how can I forget those wonderful days."

Maryam continued talking to her aunt and uncle, and Raya's thoughts again drifted in the warm late afternoon sun. In her mind's eye she saw herself as a young woman, going to the door of her areesh to welcome the group of neighbours' children who came every day to sit with her and learn the Quran. How she had enjoyed those calm quiet times with the sound of the beautiful words echoing through the room. And she had been very successful with her teaching – so many children had come. The image of her mother came to her mind; how she missed her even after all these years. She had been so strong in her life and values and religion. It was her mother who had insisted that Raya learn to read the Quran. She took her to a lady in the neighbourhood who taught the Quran. Raya was a quick learner and by the time she was 15 she was proficient at reading and writing and had finished learning the Quran. Her mother had seen Raya's teaching and leadership potential when Raya was still very young. She had also insisted that Raya gain an education at a time when very few girls did that.

"Thanks be to God" thought Raya. "She was the person who helped focus my life in its direction."

Raya broke into the conversation, addressing her sister-in-law. "I was just thinking about Umi and those days in Shindagha before everyone discovered Dubai," she said.

"Yes. I remember your mother well," replied Fatma. "She was an amazing woman, very strong to cope alone with all of you young children when your father was away pearl diving. And she was always very generous to her family members – she exemplified the Islamic way of life and Arabic hospitality."

"Yes," replied Mohamed, Raya's brother-in-law, "the dalla was always brewing coffee when we visited her house and the dalla was ready on the tray with the dish of tamur."

"And I can still smell the fish cooking in the tanoor," added his wife. "Our food was simple then but so tasty – white rice, fish, goats' milk and tea or water. And do you remember how we used to go to the souk to buy the fresh fruits that arrived from overseas on the ships?"

"Things have changed a lot in Dubai since then," commented Raya. "Life is so busy and fast now and there are so many people from other countries here now. When I was a young woman our hard work and effort revolved around the fishing season, the pearling season and date harvesting. The things I was expected to do would relate to these seasons. During the date harvest the men were out pearling and I had to take responsibility for managing both the harvest and bringing up the children. However, when the men were around we were more involved in the community social life For example, in the morning we regularly made casual visits to neighbors and then there were the more formal visits in the afternoon where we would enjoy a meal of harees, balaleet, bajela, and khemeer."

"And the Friday breakfasts were so special when all the family were together." her sister-in-law excitedly added.

Her sister's comments transported Raya back forty years to those times and could almost hear the singing and ululating in the women's majlis. She recalled how in those times – before the current generation of oil wealth and rapid development and change – there was a greater level of freedom for women than now because husbands and fathers were often working away from the home or for long periods at sea women needed to leave the home to shop for food and see to their children's needs. It was also common for women to assist their neighbours with childcare or household duties. Whilst they covered, women typically also wore a burqa which is not common practice now. As she observed her sister's beautiful Milan-designed abaya and crystal-embossed shayla, she remembered how in those days women typically wore a colourful thobe and headscarf. Now the abaya and shayla are objects of highly designed fashion for Emirati women.

She recalled how then the traditionally large and well established families lived in a large, central house or compound of buildings which were surrounded by walls to protect those inside from prying eyes. The families' children played traditional games such as al saglah, al meryeihana and al qharareef between houses and it was not uncommon to see their abandoned toys strewn along the sides of the private family roads. She could still hear the laughter of her aunts' children as they played umm al lal around the compound. There were family members everywhere and the children grew up in a caring and safe environment.

"All we had to do was call out to each other or stroll a little way and we would be at our relatives' houses," she thought. "I was always at my mother's, cousin's, niece's or aunt's place. Those were the days," she sighed.

In the past there were walled villas where several generations might live together in a large villa with separate majlis for the male and female family members. Children played behind the walls of villas built to accommodate the extended family. Now, whilst walled villas are common, the walls are higher with security to ensure privacy. Some Emiratis also now live in apartment blocks that line the Dubai skyline.

She recalled the many festive occasions during those years when the women would gather together to henna their hands and nails, decorating them with the most beautiful and ornate patterns to mark a niece's engagement, the birth of a child, a wedding in the community of the return of family and friends from the Haj. They were and still are the most wonderful of celebrations for the family and community.

In many ways the community then seemed much closer and there were many opportunities to privately celebrate with each other to reaffirm relationships through feasting, giving gifts and generally spending time together. This was the same when a community member passed away.

Nowadays though, it is not uncommon for the young men to celebrate their own occasions in public favoring restaurants and cafes. It is far more common for young people, to prefer mobile technology to communicate. Spending time with their older relatives is far less common. The communal extended family meal is still such an important tradition only now you are less likely to hear singing and ululating in the women's majlis and singing or poetry recitations in the men's.

Maryam's uncle laughed at the comment she had made. "You know in those days your father and I were usually away from home for long periods when we were pearl diving" he said.

"Yes, it wasn't easy being responsible for our children's upbringing alone," his wife joined in.

Raya smiled. "I remember those days, sitting by the manaz and rocking it as the baby slept, all the time thinking – how can I manage this? How can I deal with the housework, the children and the teaching? I had to lead my small family and lead the children's education while my husband was away and it was a big challenge."

"But do you remember when baba came home?" said Maryam to her mother, thinking about her father. "Us kids were always so excited to see him and he brought special sweets and canned juice. They were unheard of in those days. We shared them with all our friends."

There was a confusion of talk and laughter as the family members shared stories about the pearl diving days.

Afrah, Raya's second daughter, strolled across to join them with two of her cousins. "What are you laughing about Umi?"

"Oh we're just reminiscing about the 'old days' in Dubai" replied her mother. As she spoke the memories flooded back to Raya and she returned to her earlier thoughts. The buildings surrounding the Heritage Village vanished from her mind and instead she saw the old family areesh, built from palm tree fronds. There were few large buildings near the corniche in the 1950s and Raya's childhood had been a simpler, quieter one in comparison to that of her grandchildren in modern Dubai. At first when she played together with the other young girls she had been rather quiet and shy. However as her education progressed she had become more aware and more confident. These traits were the genesis of her later leadership, when she was aware of the importance of helping the children in the community become educated and had the confidence to take on that role in her own home.

From the corner of her eye Raya caught sight of a fanar swinging from the ceiling of one of the stalls. It took her back to the first Ramadan after her marriage when her husband was home with her and the family, taking a break from the hard work of pearl diving. She recalled the feeling of community and sharing as the neighbours knocked on doors before they heard the adhan bringing food ready to share for iftar after the maghgrib prayer. The whole family went to the mosque in the evening for taraweeh and then Raya and her husband would sit with the children and talk with them about the spirit of Ramadan – "when you feel the 'bite' of hunger you can feel what it is like for those less fortunate who suffer from this." Those were such special and very happy times for her.

Raya switched back to the present as she heard her brother talking.

"Do you remember the electric fans everywhere in the downtown shops then, and the wind-towers which were so common in those days? I still remember the noise of the generators too as we didn't get electricity until the 60s. That made a big difference when we could use air-conditioning."

"I remember it being very hot in the summer," said Raya, "but we didn't seem to notice it as much. I do remember going out of the city and up to the sand dunes in the summer because the humidity was lower there than by the coast. The whole family lived in tents. It was great fun for us children. We had big swings to play on and we slept on the sand in the evenings. The air was always cooler at night in the desert and we enjoyed the breeze among the sand dunes."

As the others continued reminiscing Raya's thoughts again flowed back to her youth. She had married in her 15th year and moved to her own areesh. It was then that her teaching role really began to develop. Her mother, having seen Raya's skill at teaching her younger sister, encouraged the neighbouring families to bring their children to Raya. Because of the respect they had for Raya's mother, families brought their children without hesitation. Raya smiled to herself as she remembered the daily routine. For six days of the week a group of boys and girls would arrive at her areesh and sit in a circle on the mat. At any time there were up to 14 children present in the room. Learning the Quran needed focus and concentration and Raya followed a particular approach to keep the children motivated and interested. She always treated them kindly and was never strict or harsh as that would have made them leave. She tried to make the learning fun and enjoyable. The children would arrive early in the morning after breakfast and study till lunchtime. Then they would go back to their homes for lunch and return for more study until sunset. Line by line, page by page the children learnt to read and memorize the Quran. Over time almost all the children completed their learning except for some of the boys who were called away to work with their fathers.

Maryam and Afra were also thinking about their mother as they stood together with Afra's husband Ahmed near the other family members.

"Do you remember the lessons with Umi?" said Afra, smiling at her husband.

"Of course," replied her husband. "That was when I first saw you. You were playing while we were studying. It was hard work for us but your mother was kind and humble and patient with us. We loved coming to be with her each day. Our minds were so clear and focused."

"I never thought of her then as a teacher leader," commented Latifa. "To me she was only my Umi. But now as a mother myself I truly understand the value of what she did. When I was old enough she insisted that I go to school. It was continuing what grandmother did for her. Because Umi was educated herself she knew the importance of education, especially for girls. I was jealous at first that my friends could stay at home and I had to go to school but now some of them are a little jealous of me because of the chances education gave me in my life."

"Yes, thanks to Umi's strength and support we have all done really well in our lives and work," reiterated Maryam.

Their uncle moved closer to join the conversation. "We were just remembering how Umi supported our education," Afra said to him. "Your mother always believed strongly in education," replied her uncle. "It wasn't easy for her as a young woman. She had three types of duties – being a mother to you children, taking a leadership role in the spiritual development of our community's children as a teacher and being a home-maker. Remember that your father was often away working in Abu Dhabi at that time, so your mother had full responsibility. It was a challenge for her at times but she was strong and demonstrated leadership in all that she did."

"I can still remember how she taught me special things and encouraged me to recite well," added Maryam. "When she thought I was good enough she gave me the chance to lead the other children while she watched. She did that with some of the other girls as well. It gave us confidence in ourselves."

"I remember when we moved from Shindagha to Jumeira – that was when Umi stopped teaching classes," said Latifa.

"But she focused on *our* education even more after that," replied her sister. "Particularly our Islamic studies. Umi was always very careful about that aspect of our education."

"Her religion has always been the cornerstone of her life," commented their uncle. "This came from her own mother. Your grandmother was highly respected in Shindagha and ladies often came to her for advice about religious matters."

"Mash'allah, and now this is what Umi does," smiled Latifa. "She gets a lot of phone calls from people in Dubai who want to speak with her about these things. Like mother like daughter. Maybe you will pick up this role when you are older, Maryam."

Maryam laughed. "Well, Umi has certainly laid the groundwork for me over the years. She is so wise – I think that wisdom is one of the most important things that I am learning from her."

"And she knows so much from the past," added Latifa. "She has an amazing memory and can recite very old poems by heart. Some of them are hundreds of years old. That is a real skill."

A little further away Raya stood and gazed around her. She enjoyed coming to Heritage Village as there was much there that reminded her of the earlier days in Shindagha. Her eyes lifted to the tall buildings in the distance.

"So much has changed," she thought. "And now my own life has come full circle. First I was a student, because my mother pushed me to get an education, then I became a teacher myself and helped other people's children. Then I became a mother and teacher to my own children and pushed *them* to get a good education and now I've become a student again, learning Arabic grammar." She smiled to herself as she reflected on how much she was enjoying the time to focus on her own learning again. All her life she had wanted to memorize the Quran and this had been her focus for the last three years. "Learning and teaching is in my blood," she thought. "I never want to stop."

Raya walked slowly across the sand to join her daughters. She was so proud of them and her other children. All those early years of challenge and hard work were worth it. Just as her own mother had started Raya on her life's path so had Raya done the same for her children.

Maryam and Afra moved towards Raya and took her hands.

"We are so proud of you, Umi," stated Maryam, smiling at her mother. "You have always been a leader for us and your other students. We may not always have agreed with you as we were growing up, but now we understand how much knowledge and wisdom you have."

"Aiwa, I agree," added Afra. "We may be educated but we still need our mother's wisdom."

"That is true," agreed Raya. "But now that my children have a university education I can also come to you for knowledge. We complete each other!"

Hand in hand with her daughters Raya strolled back to the other family members. In the background the sounds of the midday adhan floated through the air and the family started towards their cars to return home.

Note

1   Heritage Village is a tourist site in Dubai that replicates some elements of earlier Dubai lifestyle.

CHAPTER 5

Raja Al Gurg

If how you lead inspires others to be more creative, learn more, take action, consider the common good and reach their full potential, it is a life well lived.

∵

Raja's legacy will have been to inspire future generations to forge a new path for themselves in their chosen fields of expertise with confidence and self belief.

Raja Al Gurg is a businesswoman who lives in Dubai (UAE). She is the Managing Director of the Easa Saleh Al Gurg Group and a Board Member of the Dubai Chamber of Commerce and Industry. Raja graduated from Kuwait University in 1977 with a degree in English Literature and served as headmistress of Zabeel Secondary School for Girls from 1978 to 1989. In 1989 she joined the Board of Directors of the Easa Saleh Al Gurg Group. In September 2003, Al Gurg, along with Sheikha Lubna Al-Qasimi, led a delegation of Dubai businesswomen to the USA-Arab Economic Forum.

ArabianBusiness.com listed Al Gurg as the fifth most powerful Arab woman in 2012 and she was selected as the Figure of the Month by the Al Waref Institute for Humanitarian Studies in September 2009. During the Third Middle East Women Achievement Awards in 2011, Raja Al Gurg was recognised with the Woman of the Year Award. She has consistently remained in the upper ranks of 100 most powerful Arab women each year and holds positions including chairperson, directorships and board memberships of numerous business and community organisations.

1   Raja's Story

Raja sat in her office high above the Dubai Creek. She had a precious few minutes to herself on a day that typically was filled with meetings and phone calls. She thrived on the workload and her friends and associates knew her personal motto well "Resting is rusting." At this moment her mind was active, thinking about the Keynote address she would make at the inaugural Arab Women and Leadership in a Global World conference in three months' time.

It was her nature to completely focus on any given task so that she was fully organized and prepared for its execution. The Conference organizers had given her a wide brief to comment on her own leadership journey and on the future for Arab women leaders in a rapidly changing world. As a role model for her children, her organization and her people in recent years Raja had spoken widely at international forums about the achievements of Arab women and was excited by another opportunity to continue this work. "Regrettably there are still too many people who think of us as neglected on the shelves, in tents or on camels" she had said to her friends. "My vision is to change this perception by helping others understand the role of women in Arab society."

Her keen mind explored possible avenues for her address. Where should she start? Should she begin with her childhood and talk about her beloved parents – how her father had instilled in her the values of hard work and self discipline together with the importance of family life, and how her mother had taught her the importance of religion and morals and what it meant to be a woman and mother? Or should she start from her university education period where in Kuwait she had learned to rely on her own skills to develop independence and self support living on a government allowance without any extra financial help? Perhaps she should commence her address by talking about her leadership development from teacher to school principal when for eleven years she had encouraged her teachers and students to strive for the best in education. She smiled to herself as she thought about how, even more than ten years after she had left education, many of her former colleagues and students still kept in touch. That was what mattered in life – the strength of long term relationships – and she still had those friendships from her childhood and beyond.

The intercom buzzed on her desk and she heard her executive secretary's voice announcing that Mr Salim Juma Ali, CEO of a local business enterprise would be present in a few minutes.

"Thank you Maria. Can you call for fresh tea please"?

The intercom again …. "And your son, Abdulla, has called to say he will be a few minutes late to join you for lunch today."

As she readied the meeting documents on her desk, Raja's thoughts turned to her family. They were her first priority and a key source of strength for her. She smiled again as she recalled once when her children were clustered on her bed and her husband had teased her, saying she was like a mother cat with her kittens. As her sons and daughters had grown she had made sure she was always there for them, protecting and guiding, and now her relationship with them was as much a friend as a mother. She looked forward to the lunch with her eldest son as he had told her he wanted to discuss something that was happening in his work. All her children were like that. They knew that they could talk about anything with her and they valued her wisdom and advice. She remembered back to when they were just small kids and had just a small amount of pocket money to spend. She had wanted them to learn responsibility and how to manage money. They understood well that, like she had done, they must become independent and work hard in their life to achieve their rewards. She remembered when the whole family had gone to Colorado to set up a flat for her eldest son to study there and he had realized he was not ready to stay on in the States while his family were in Dubai. Raja did not force him to stay as she knew her son well and appreciated that he was a family man. She had supported his decision to focus on family and study in the UAE instead.

Her children's education was a top priority. For Raja, a good education was essential. She had taken a keen interest in her children's learning and attended parent-teacher meetings with a note book in hand to record the feedback which she later discussed with her children. She had communicated her high expectations and reminded her children, nieces and nephews that nothing comes easily in life. She always reminded them that it was hard work that enables you to reach your goals.

Raja's thoughts flowed spontaneously to her father. He was a self made success story. He had started with a small business, built that business into a hugely successful family business, moved into politics and then for 18 years held the honorable position of Ambassador for the United Arab Emirates in the United Kingdom and Ireland. As such he also became the Dean of the Diplomatic Corps of London. Just as her children trusted her advice she was the same with his. He was a role model for her.

"I've really inherited his genes," she reflected, thinking about how the family's business interests had continued to prosper since he had turned over full responsibility to her. She had sought his opinion and advice on everything in the early years as she gained knowledge and experience. She still always turned to him first for advice, and looked forward to speaking with him and keeping him informed about her decisions and she valued every minute of their time shared together. It wasn't always easy for a woman in the male-dominated world of Arabic business and there were many times when she had to be sensitive about others' expectations of her. Raja was not concerned about the appearance of remaining quiet and thinking through a situation before giving her opinion. In order to make effective decisions she wanted to give them the required time and thought necessary for them to be effective ones. And yet there were some rare occasions when Raja's silence was because she still needed more information and consultation in order to be sure she had all the necessary facts. Her father had advised her that during these times as a woman in a large group of powerful men it was important to have all the information at hand. She remembered him advising "When you find yourself in meetings like that and you are not sure you have enough necessary information, just take your time. You have two ears and one tongue so listen more than you talk on those occasions." His advice had helped her a lot but she still wanted to talk more with him about how to navigate the sometimes frustrating social barriers that made it harder for her to approach government ministers than her male counterparts.

She reflected on how she now gives advice to young women entrepreneurs. Just yesterday she had addressed such a group; "Get involved with your companies; do not sit back relaxing at the side lines. The youth of this land have been born with golden spoons in their mouths. Think well about how you can seize this opportunity and challenge the way we live, learn and behave. The youth of this great nation need to be leaders in their homes and businesses. Be sure of yourselves. Learn confidence and what is appropriate for the context. Do not be overly concerned about appearances; be concerned about who you are."

Her thoughts drifted further back to when she had first started in the family business. It was a big jump from being a graduate in English literature, without a small business background, to taking a management role in a well established and complex company, but she had taken the perspective that the company was like a 'university' where she could study and learn from others as she grew into her role. She clearly recalled a feeling that she had to 'prove' herself – to show to employees that she was not in the position as the owner's daughter, but that she had skills that were needed in the business. Her father had told her that it would take ten years to 'learn the business' and at first she had thought to herself, "Why is he trying to put me off"? However after the ten years had passed she went back and thanked him because his perspective had pushed her to take the time and effort to learn 'from scratch' every aspect of the business.

She smiled to herself as she remembered her first choice was to focus on the interior design and furniture section of the company, and how the employees had been initially surprised to see her helping with loading and unloading goods and checking inventories. From the very beginning of her career she had always had a very hands on approach. From the start of her time in the family business she was on site every day, in the showrooms and factories, and encouraged this in her own children as they learned about life and leadership and the family business.

This had really helped her to understand the nature of the business, the needs and concerns of employees and how to deal with people at all levels. One of her strengths was that she could look at relationships from both sides. In the Ministry of Education she had been an employee and she knew how it felt to be an employee. In her principal's role she could understand the teachers' perspective as well as what it meant to be the 'boss.' Such understanding had translated easily into the business setting. Looking back, it seemed strange now that at first she hadn't even been sure how to read a balance sheet. As was her way, when faced with something she wanted to know more about, she went to an expert. She had asked the accountant to help her.

And now all these years later she felt at the peak of her life. All her efforts and giving to society were paying off. The company was thriving; she was an executive member of a number of boards; she held office in business associations; she was a highly respected member of the community and well known for her own leadership. Her kindness and humility were also well known and she was always ready to help others.

She then turned to the letter on her desk. She had only just received it and was thrilled to read that she was the recipient of the Leadership Excellence award from the Gulf Cooperation Council (GCC) Chamber of Commerce. It was in recent years that she had begun to reap the rewards of her efforts. She had built up her image through the way she consistently lived her life through her behavior and continuous professional and life learning. She had taken advantage of the many opportunities life had presented her. Her greatest opportunity was her father being a lifelong guide and support for her. She thought too about her organization. She was surrounded by experienced people from whom she had continually learnt.

She had worn so many different hats –in the business world and in her tireless work for the Dubai Women Council (DWC). She could hardly believe it had been seven years since the inception of the DWC. She thought back to how encouraging H.H. Sheikh Mohammed had been when the International Monetary Fund first came to Dubai. It was naturally a big deal and even though DWC was only six or seven people they were very keen to be involved in some way. Raja was keen to support this prestigious three day event and offered to escort Mrs Wolfson. Her professionalism, punctuality, communicative ability and initiative made a big impression on the participants and on H.H. Sheikh Mohammad who as a result asked fifteen women from the DWC to join the men for a conference in Detroit. From 8am–10pm the fifteen women gladly attended sessions, participated in workshops, meetings, luncheons and dinners. At the end of the conference the women wanted to thank H.H. Sheikh Mohammad but it was he who said he wanted to in fact thank them for their punctuality and attendance at all sessions and for demonstrating the achievements of UAE women and presenting such a wonderful image of UAE women to the world.

It was from that point on that Raja took the initiative to travel the world and challenge the image of Arab women as underutilized, marginalized and discriminated against. "We have changed this stereotype of UAE women," she thought proudly. "And yet after visits to the USA, Europe, Japan, Australia,

Canada and many more countries it seems high time that others make the visit to the UAE to see our achievements."

Since 2006 over 40 female delegates had visited the UAE to see what is happening for themselves. Because of Raja's leadership experience she was called on regularly to address international audiences. Yet, still she understood there were subtleties of social expectations of her community and the challenges she faced in becoming fully accepted in the way her male colleagues took for granted. There was still work to be done.

Maria's voice broke into her thoughts.

"Mr Salim Juma Ali is here. Shall I send him in?"

Three months later Raja sat quietly on the stage while Professor Julie Donaldson, the new Provost of Zayed University began speaking "Your royal highness, your excellencies, honored guests, ladies and gentlemen. It is a pleasure and a privilege for me to present our keynote speaker for this inaugural Arab Women and Leadership in a Global World conference. She is someone who is very well known to many of you in the audience but allow me to take a few minutes to highlight her work ...."

Raja felt relaxed and ready for this. Her Powerpoint slides had been finalized a week ago and she had practiced the timing of her address. Earlier she had met with the technicians to load her slides and to ensure that everything was in order. She never left things to chance.

As she waited and gazed out at the packed auditorium she let her thoughts flow. There were many familiar faces she could see. There was her father and her children sitting with the dignitaries. Sir Easa Al Gurg's head was bent towards his youngest grandson who was smiling and whispering something in his ear. Her daughters, Sara and Amal, and her niece, Fatma, were sitting together engrossed in whispered conversation. Further back Raja could see three of her oldest friends, Rashida Badri, Fatma Al Marri and Rafia Abbas sitting together and smiling towards her. She had known them since she was at school and then throughout her time at the Ministry of Education. And there on the left were more friends from the business community including her trusted ally Faiza. There too was a group of teachers from her days at Zabeel Secondary – now moving through the ranks to seniority as principals and administrators. She looked intently to find Amal – her long lost and recently found friend from university days in Kuwait and Oxford. "Thank God through Amal's son-in-law we finally made contact again after all those years I searched for her," thought Raja. Yes, there she was in the third row.

Sir Easa finished the whispered conversation with his grandson and turned back to the stage, observing his daughter with quiet pride as she waited. How right he had been to bring her into the family business over a decade ago. Some of his colleagues had expressed doubt that she could handle the cut and thrust of business in a largely male domain but his trust in her had been implicit. He knew his daughter very well and had watched her grow from a strong young adult, eager to learn and travel, to the steady and mature woman she was now. She was truly a daughter to be proud of – loving and respectful and ready to learn everything he could teach her about business, life and leadership but at the same time an effective decision-maker in her own right who had continued to build the family business into the highly successful business that it was today. Not for Raja was there any prominent show of wealth and status like some other well known families, but rather a quiet determination to hold on to the important values that had sustained her through her life and instilled in those early childhood years and beyond. He was particularly pleased with how she had upheld his strong beliefs in balancing the rights of employees and the company.

Her door was always open to employees and in response their service and loyalty were evident. Some of them had been with the company for more than thirty five years. Sir Easa recalled the time recently when rents had increased almost sixty percent. The company had held staff rents at the same level and carried the burden of the extra costs until they could build accommodation for their employees. No other company had done that to his knowledge, but the decision was a clear reflection of the values he and Raja lived by.

He glanced fondly at his grandchildren. They too had grown into fine young people assisted by their mother's deep love, wisdom and skill and were now making their own assured way in the world.

Raja's daughter Amal was also watching her mother proudly and intently, thinking about her mother's achievements over the years. "Despite all her responsibilities she has always put us first," Amal thought to herself. "Now I can really appreciate her way with us as children and in the way our parents chose to raise us as a family. Whilst my mother was strict about many things, which was important, she also helped us arrive at very good decisions. Sometimes it really felt like a bit of a burden at first as we knew we had to make decisions ourselves and be accountable for them. Nevertheless, later we realized the value of her advice and guidance. I want to bring up *my* children in this way."

Amal's brother Abdulla sat back in his chair and watched his mother with the utmost respect and love. Such an amazing woman. As an adult he could see much more the benefits of her particular and special approach to life. Self discipline and structure was always important to her and he knew from his own work experience that this led to success.

Abdulla snapping out of his thoughts about his own work life prior to recently joining the family business, smiled inwardly as he recalled how some of his mother's former students had joked with him about her disciplined approach – "You're Raja's son! How did you survive? He understood that his mother strived for perfection in all that she did and while sometimes that wasn't easy to deal with as he was growing up, he knew now that her unconditional love, wisdom and clear guidance had built a secure environment for all of the family. "She's so organized – always thinks five steps in advance," Abdulla reflected. "I'm really starting to think like her!"

Rashida, Fatma and Rafia commented quietly to each other as the Provost's introduction continued. They did not need to hear her words as they had grown up with Raja through school in to their early years at university and then through their work as teacher leaders together and they knew her strengths and abilities very well.

In hushed tones to the others Rafia said, "You know if I had to sum up Raja in one word, I'd choose the word 'respect.' She has so much self respect."

"Yes," agreed Rashida, "and she always shows respect for others, no matter what their age or circumstance in life …."

"And that's why she is respected in return," Fatma said. "I'm so glad we've kept in contact over the years. It isn't as easy these days as our lives are so busy, but Raja is one of the rocks who anchors our relationship." The others nodded in full support but very aware of the fact that Raja was about to speak at any point.

Amal was quiet as she gazed lovingly at her friend. How amazing that they had found each other again after more than 30 years. How Amal loved everything about Raja then just as she stood before so many now. Raja was no different than Amal remembered her when they were young university students enjoying each other's company, catching the train together from Oxford to Paddington to shop and eat together in London. Raja was serious and focused on her study but always ready to join her friend for some fun and relaxation after the work was done. And now in this recent renewal of their friendship they had hugged and cried and laughed together as though the separation had never happened. Amal felt humble when she thought how Raja, now holding such an important position in the UAE, had welcomed her and cared for her after so many years and everything that they had been through separately but particularly her own life as " the family went through hell in Palestine." "That's real friendship and love and I was truly grateful for her kindness" she thought as she remembered how they came together again. "Our names both mean 'hope' and Raja has renewed my hope in life after all this time." Amal sighed and as the tears welled up Faiza, Raja's friend and colleague from the Business Women's Council, caught her eye and smiled.

As Faiza, vice-president of the Business Women's Council, looked at Amal and marveled at her and Raja's reunion, it reminded her of the time when she and Raja were in Egypt on a business trip. Raja had said "Let's find my old music teacher." She'd kept her number for years and sure enough they had found her and paid a visit. How like Raja – always thinking about others and maintaining her connections and love for people over time.

These were important leadership skills in her work with the DWC and other organisations in Dubai. Faiza admired Raja's skill at giving advantage to others and negotiating around any disadvantage. She had proven herself well able to hold her place in the complexity of the Arab world of business and commerce. Faiza recalled how Raja had come to the business world with a reputation as a strong school leader who could face any challenge. What had impressed Faiza and other business associates was Raja's phenomenal knowledge and ability to get things done. In Council she could lead a discussion and respond to questions on any topic, even at short notice. She was always well prepared but in addition she had a manner with people that made them feel valued and cared for. It was uncanny the way the tone and atmosphere in a room changed when Raja walked in – she was hugely respected by both women and men.

Further back in the auditorium, Aisha, Maryam and Shahla conferred softly together as they waited for Raja's address. They had been colleagues alongside Raja when she was principal some twelve years previously and were all now deputy principals.

"I can still remember the atmosphere in the school when we worked with Raja," commented Aisha.

"Yes, we were really like a family," added Shahla. "I remember that several teachers left the school when Raja left because they couldn't imagine working with any other principal" Her door was always open to teachers, students and parents. The students really loved her – she was such a role model to them."

"I recall that she was very young when she took up the principal position" said Maryam. "She was handpicked for that role because of her ability. It must have been a challenge for her as many of the teachers were a lot older."

"But she was really effective in the job," responded Aisha. "She was confident, innovative and supportive of the teachers. She was a perfectionist and that kept us all working towards a high standard but she was also such a hard worker herself that nobody complained."

"I think Raja is a work addict," laughed Shahla. "But what I also remember is the respect that everyone had for her. She was an amazing communicator and still is! She is polite, straightforward and honest. And so persuasive! As principal of Zabeel School, parents, teachers and students responded so well to her communication style. I've tried very hard in my own school to interact with my teachers and students like she did with us. In those fourteen years we all learned so much from each other. We were a team that really cared about the individuals in it and we had some great individual and collective successes as a result."

"I'm really looking forward to what she's going to say tonight," said Maryam. "She provides such an incredible example of leadership."

In these last few minutes Raja reflected on her own life achievements and those of her family, community and country. She had established herself as a respected female leader in the UAE through hard work, determination and creating a supportive environment for herself, her family and her employees. Only that morning her youngest daughter had asked if she could attend an international event with her. When Raja asked why, Sara had said it was because she wanted to see what it was like .... "I want to be known as you are Mama." Raja smiled lovingly as she recalled her advice to Sara, "You must have your own approach and persona. I will always be there to support you but you need to stand on your own."

She thought about a famous poet's words ... failure for a country is eating what you don't plant and drinking what you don't make. She looked at her audience and thought ... "We need to be leaders in production, education, health and training. Why don't we trust our own doctors, educators? Why do we send our children to private schools? Why don't we improve our educational system? Leadership should be included from early on in a child's education. Personality is built early on and it's in early childhood that we need to concentrate more. Family life and schooling influence who we are and who we become in later life."

Raja then turned her thoughts once again to her children. They had had a normal upbringing despite her family's wealth and position. She and her husband had worked as a team and consistently tried to ensure that their children understood the value of hard work and money. She had brought them up knowing what was in their own pockets and she was very proud of who they had become.

"... And now I ask our keynote speaker to begin her address. Mrs Raja Al Gurg!" She stood up and began moving confidently towards the podium. The Provost sat down as the sound of applause rang out around the conference centre. Raja moved closer to the podium and paused while it died down. "Bismillah, Rahmane Rahim ...," she began as the title of her address displayed on the screen behind her. 'Arab Women and Leadership: A Continuing Journey.'

"I would like to begin my talk today by acknowledging the incredible support of my father, husband and children. They are my reason d'etre. I, too, wish to acknowledge the inspirational leadership of His Highness Sheikh Mohammed Bin Rashid Al Maktoum, UAE Prime Minister and Vice-President, and Ruler of Dubai.

You could have heard a pin drop in the auditorium as Raja began her speech.

CHAPTER 6

Rafia Abbas

Change is the needed reality. Teamwork is the strategy.

∴

Rafia's legacy is to have been a pioneer in the introduction of innovative learner-centered teaching practices, first through her work as a classroom teacher and then through her leadership role as a Ministry of Education supervisor where she influenced supported significant changes in the professional development of teachers of English and their classroom culture.

Rafia Abbas is currently retired. Previously she worked as an English teacher and English supervisor in the Dubai Education Zone, and a deputy-principal in a prestigious private school in Dubai She has been the first at many things. She was the first person to win the Hamdan Award in 1998 for Distinctive Academic Performance in her supervisor's role. She was also the first Ministry of Education English Supervisor to be a member of the international organization TESOL Inc. She was honored with her colleague Rashida Badri for presenting an innovative workshop at the International TESOL Conference in Utah in 2002. She is an innovator and distinguished educational leader who has impacted the Dubai educational system in significant ways during her career particularly through the introduction of learner-centered pedagogy.

1 Rafia's Story

1.1 *A Typical School Day*
The twenty fifth of March, two thousand and five was just another normal day at the school or so we thought until the troubling shouting and complaining erupted. Students scattered and administrators came running. The man was beside himself with anger and yet when Rafia appeared she calmly and without hesitation invited him into her office. Her lifelong friend, Rashida, came out close behind Rafia, embraced her friend and said she would see her later on. The irate man was ushered into Rafia's office and she closed the door behind them.

© KONINKLIJKE BRILL NV, LEIDEN, 2018 | DOI 10.1163/9789004372948_006

Layla and I glanced at each other and I decided to wait nearby in case Rafia should need me, although I knew that I would undoubtedly not be needed. She had this marvelous way about her. She just seemed to be able to put anyone at ease and she was so persuasive. Others happily did what Rafia wanted. As I waited I thought about all the different times I had learned from Rafia.

After about half an hour Rafia's door opened again. I thought I could hear laughter and had to check myself as surely the angry shouting had not turned so quickly to laughter. Sure enough as they left Rafia's office they were both all smiles. Layla and I smiled too. It was in fact a typical day as Rafia seemed to always manage to turn negative situations around. She managed to help others see solutions. Her kindness and concern for others seemed limitless and I saw her as such a wonderful role model. She was able to identify a person's strengths and then work with them to encourage them to do the best that they can.

"So Sara," Layla said, "It seems like everything turned out OK with Mr. Ahmed."

"Yes," I smiled. "Rafia has worked her magic again."

Just then Rafia walked around the corner and hugged us warmly and smiled. "Who would like a cup of tea?" she offered. "I could sure use one."

Layla and I smiled and followed Rafia to the teacher's room. Rafia could easily have stayed in her own office and taken her tea there but she never did. She was constantly out and about talking with the teachers, students and parents trying to find out how things were going around the school and how she could be of help.

This morning was no exception and she was curious to find out how my Math class had gone. Just the day before she had offered to help me with it and we had discussed the plan in great detail. She has observed me teaching a few times now and I have always received such useful suggestions from her. She has a different way of thinking about teaching and learning. She believes that as teachers teach children, the children also teach you something in return.

I thought back to the time when I had had a student who was struggling with Math. Rafia's attitude to life had rubbed off on me from that day with Asma. She made us realize that life is a learning experience and that nothing is impossible in life. Asma seemed to be daydreaming all the time in my classes. One day the child's father came to see me and told me that everything I taught his daughter was repeated at home with great pride. I was surprised as this meant Asma had in fact learned it. There and then I decided to differentiate more during the lessons. The more time I invested in this child's learning the more I learned about myself as well as Asma's needs and interests.

When I recounted what this event had taught me to Rafia she had commented that naturally students need individual attention at times and each child has different needs and learning preferences. In fact Rafia and I had discussed this after one of the lessons she had observed me teach. At the time I really didn't understand the importance of her comments. It was typically like this with Rafia. It was only later that I realized how useful her questioning and suggestions were. When studying for my Masters we looked at various learning theories and as I read more and more about Gardner's multiple intelligence theory I remembered Rafia. Her teaching philosophy and in fact her whole leadership approach seemed to draw on this theory.

We had our tea together but before Rafia could finish hers a member of staff had called her back to her office about another insistent parent who was adamant about a problem she felt needed to be solved. "Even a clock that doesn't work is right twice a day," she laughed.

"How can she do that?" asked Afra.

"What do you mean?" asked Layla.

"I mean, Rafia got that guy to calm down and even leave with a smile on his face," she said.

"For me Rafia has this amazing way of helping people, making you feel empowered, like you are equals. I mean, I do not feel as if I am her subordinate because she talks to you at a level that you can understand and that makes you feel like you have something to contribute," I confided.

"Yes, I agree completely," said Layla. "Rafia makes everyone feel important and unique. She does it quietly with humility and yet she is so charismatic."

"In what way do you mean?" asked Alya.

"Well, as a Vice Principal Rafia looks at situations and then adopts the necessary style to achieve her intended goals. Sometimes she delegates and sometimes she is more authoritative. She knows how to get things done and she is a great communicator. She listens and gets to know the style of the person she is speaking with and adopts a style that would work best with them. She also involves others to get different opinions. She keeps her word and honors her promises," I said.

"It's the way she says, yes we can with that engaging smile of hers," Layla said. "She has a way of influencing people. She's the type of person you can't say no to. She still has all her friends ... some go back more than thirty years."

"Yes, people are attracted to her. She's always so positive. She can make you feel more positive even when things aren't going that well," said Layla. "Rafia regularly reminds us how important it is to feel good about ourselves. You know how she advises us to leave our problems at home so that we can pass on those positive feelings and energy to our students and colleagues at the school? I can remember one example of this so clearly. When I first started here at the school, nine years ago, and I was having a lot of trouble managing a class of mine and Rafia instead of making me feel bad by commenting on what I was not doing suggested that I try to engage the students by being positive about learning. She recommended project based learning with the class. At first I could not see why she had changed the subject methodology. It was only as I really started exploring Project Based Learning that I realized how useful it was for managing learning and therefore managing behaviour ... because it became about the students' energy ... along with mine ... controlling the learning. There was no need for strict rules and regulations anymore. Then there was that time she suggested a 12 year old lead my class or the time she said to those parents that the students needed more activities and games, not less. Remember Sara? I could go on and on."

"Yes, how keen Rafia was for us to try out better ways of teaching and assessing," Sara recalled. Then she said, "Rafia is able to communicate ideas in a way that students and teachers understand and we learn from her example. She is a true pioneer in changing the ways children are being taught in this country. She encourages learner independence and critical thinking. When we try new things we are encouraged to celebrate our successes and this makes us even keener to excel I think," Rafia's words rang in my ears, 'Your success is my success.'

"I remember when one of the teachers complained about 'having to teach the curriculum' and Rafia paused and looked at us all intently," I continued.

"But we are teaching people, we are not teaching curriculum" she emphasized passionately. "Because we are teaching people we need to develop a rapport with the students, create emotional relationships with them and reach out to them. The best way to engage students and help them learn is by developing trusting relationships with them."

I recalled that all of us nodded but I could tell that for most teachers this was an epiphany for them.

"So it sounds like she was very much involved in the instructional side of things from the very beginning then," Alya observed. "No wonder she was the first supervisor to win the Hamdan Award."

"Absolutely. She was different and stood out. For example, after several personal visits and classroom observations, Rafia was invited by the Cultural Attache of the American Embassy, to participate in a one month long multi-regional exchange program – the International Visitors Program – on English language learning and teaching in the USA. She also received a personal letter from the UAE Ambassador inviting her to visit him in Washington.

She had a particular philosophy of teaching that focused on the individual learner. She believed that every child could learn and that all children deserved to learn in a safe, secure and stress free environment. She encouraged a move away from a focus on teaching the curriculum and instead supported the use of learner-centered activities and games at a time when these things were almost unheard of in Dubai government schools. She was a risk taker and innovator that advocated motivating children to learn English through engaging, meaningful and authentic learning. However, 'many thought she was from another planet' because she challenged the status quo. Remember that time she adapted the concept of the open air classroom for her classes? She asked the principal for permission to take the class outside to teach them a song and the principal thought she was mad! But Rafia did it and the children loved it. Oh, and remember that day she took the grade 12 class outside to plant trees for the unit on the environment? The class was so engrossed in their learning that along with Rafia they did not hear the Head of the Dubai Zone approaching. You could have heard a pin drop and the Head watched on in amazement. How had Rafia done that?

When Rafia finally noticed the Head she smiled and held out the shovel and a tree for him to plant. It was an amazing and moving sight to see. Rafia had to remain determined as she modelled best practice and persuaded those around her. She had to demonstrate resilience and perseverance over and over again to have her voice heard. She constantly reminded teachers of the importance of creating a relaxed classroom atmosphere to help children overcome their concerns and inhibitions about language learning. It was ok for children to make grammar and pronunciation mistakes because this meant that they were learning. She continually demonstrated cooperative learning strategies for teachers and encouraged them to pair students in ways that enabled children to learn from each other. She advocated inquiry learning way before it became the new way to teach and in her own classes she adopted a learner centered curriculum that enabled children to choose the activities and topics that interested them. Remember, some of us were quite uncertain about what she was suggesting we do and so she introduced teacher visits and soon we all became very comfortable visiting each other's classes. We learned so much from these observations. And it was a powerful way of creating a community of learners. It was no longer just the head of the department that visited a class for evaluative purposes. We all did it," I said.

"Rafia understands the responsibility and the power that teachers and educational leaders hold. She encouraged us all to see how we could shape and mold our future society by giving the children in our care the very best to enable them to think critically for themselves and develop their capacities. Rather than labelling a child as 'lazy,' 'ADHD,' 'unmotivated' and so on, Rafia reminds us of the importance of our roles as teachers and facilitators of societal change. She reminds us always that we have the most important profession in the country and we can make a real difference to the lives of our younger generations."

"Yes, it seems as though she really tries to develop all those around her, children and adults alike," observed Alya.

"For sure. Rafia continually fostered team work and team development. Remember Ian Percy's Eleven Commandments for an Enthusiastic Team that she shared with us all?"

"Yes," said Layla. "I still remember the ones that seemed to underpin all that we did:

> Have fun!
> Do everything with enthusiasm.
> Help each other be right, not wrong.
> Look for ways to make new ideas work – not for reasons they won't.
> Take pride in each other's successes.
> Speak positively about each other and your school at every opportunity.
> Act with initiative and courage."

"When Rafia became a supervisor she used her positive energy to affect positive change in the teachers and their teaching. She constantly reminded us in her words and deeds that she was there to help the teachers grow. Prior to Rafia's supervision, there had been a great deal of fear of supervisors because they were perceived as policing the teachers. Remember teachers were very nervous of supervisor visits because their experiences indicated that supervisors were there to focus on the negatives? Rafia used to say 'every teacher has positives and I would like to focus on those first.' As a result of Rafia's focus first on the things that were working and helping children learn, teachers began to really enjoy her supervision and the professional learning opportunities that she facilitated. It was Rafia who introduced peer coaching and our buddy system. So many had the chance to develop as a result of her efforts – students, teachers, staff and administrators," said Layla.

She went on, "Rafia used to work with her team of English supervisors, on the most amazing programs for the children. The 30th National Day Celebration was a huge success as a result of the teamwork and collaboration of supervisors, principals, teachers, parents and students. I can still see those bright young children's faces smiling with pride and joy as they performed their co-written play "Emirates We Love You." They then sang the song, that Rafia had helped write, so beautifully.

Rafia didn't take all the credit for her work. Instead, all the presentations, papers, reports and proposals she led went out under the Inspectorate of English, Dubai Zone. She wanted the credit to be the whole team's. She was always the first to acknowledge others good work. She often gave the credit for her own excellent work to others in support of them. She was an integral figure in establishing Dubai Education Zone's yearly awards program where English language teachers were presented with certificates of honor for their good work. I can safely say that I am in the leadership position I am now in because of her. I have learned a lot from her in these nine years. Even my social relationships and networks are totally different as a result of her influence and example. I mean, I still have my own identity but the way I approach people is as a result of Rafia's example," Layla reflected.

"I heard that Rafia was also very involved in TESOL Arabia as an organizer of and contributor to workshops?" said Alya.

"Yes, one of them that she presented with Rashida Badri was so well received by the participants because it was a hands on workshop on ways to design creative classroom activities to help teachers make learning English more enjoyable for children. It was so practical and we all left the session ready to try out all the good ideas they had suggested. Remember in those days Rafia and Rashida were known as 'the two Rs' because they did so much together. They were collaborative leaders who combined their individual efforts which resulted in a team to be reckoned with. They were an exceptional team and it was obvious in all that they did," I said.

"They both seem so very kind," observed Alya.

"That's for sure. Although I must say sometimes Rafia ends up being a bit too kind. I have seen her taken advantage of by more opportunistic types and so we try to watch out for her. Sometimes she just needs to say 'no.'" I said.

"I agree," Layla said. "Look, I'll give you an example Alya. There was a time about four years back when Rafia was extremely sick and we asked her if she had made an appointment to see the doctor. Remember Sara?"

I nodded. "Yes. She hadn't made the appointment, had she? I mean, if my son was ill she would call the doctor herself."

"She carries on and drives herself harder but with the staff she is the opposite."

At this point, Ghassan entered and we invited him to join Alya, Layla and I at the table and he poured himself some tea. As he sat down he asked if we had heard what Rafia had managed this morning with the owner of the Games Zone across the road.

We smiled and told him that we had in fact been telling Alya a bit about Rafia's leadership style.

"She's a special person that's for sure. As a close family friend I have seen how she is with her children as well. She has instilled honesty and a love of learning in them. So many mothers would visit Rafia asking her what she was doing to make her kids excel in their learning." Ghassan laughed. "I mean, some of them even asked what Rafia was feeding her kids."

We all smiled.

"Rafia loved books and book shops. Her husband did too." Ghassan said. "When the family travelled abroad Rafia used to buy books, books and more books. She was always looking for current best practices in teaching, learning and assessment. She welcomed change and would often try out the ideas on her own kids. She was also so very creative and had a real 'hands on' approach with her own children and encouraged that in all classrooms. Her creative thinking meant that she was always trying to apply new and modern education techniques to her own innovative projects."

"Yes, I can see that in the way she still is today," Alya said. "I mean, she has been in education for twenty three years or so now right? We can all learn from her example."

"She's seen so many fads and changes and through it all she has been consistently focused on the individual be it students, teachers or parents. Her concerns for the whole person have meant that she has always had learning at the forefront of her learner-centered approaches and she truly believes in making a difference to children's lives and society's progress," I said.

We had all begun walking back to our respective areas and the conversation stopped once we got into the school's lobby. As I sat back in my chair and checked my email I saw there was an email from Rafia's daughter. We sometimes met up for coffee. Amal was a real credit to her mum. I thought about the ways Rafia had fostered a love of learning in her kids. They were all such caring and honest children and Rafia's influence on them was everywhere. I would love to be like that with my own two daughters. Rafia believes in empowering others and she is keen to help people. She is consultative, inclusive and even handed with decision making and typically involves and listens to others before making a decision. She was this way even with her children. I hope I can be the kind of leader and mother that Rafia is and that my children turn out like hers. I clicked on Amal's email and began reading.

In the meantime Rafia had been busily engaged with a parent who was concerned about her daughter's level of English language development. This parent had particularly wanted to hear Rafia's perspective because Rafia was extremely well known in the field as someone who found ways of engaging children in meaningful learning that led to student success. She had been a risk taker from way back and was no stranger to change. Given her willingness to try out new ideas and create new and different ways of English language learning she had had much success with her own classes. Keen to share her new learning and given her charisma and influence, soon she had had very traditional teachers trying out innovative methods of teaching, learning and assessment that would have once seemed unheard of. This was why the parent was here.

As Mariam sipped on her tea, she thanked Rafia again for making the time to see her unexpectedly today. Rafia smiled graciously as Mariam continued.

"I have observed your caring, collaborative and communicative style with teachers and the support you have from the school principal, Ms Rafia, and you clearly focus on mentoring and coaching your teachers," Mariam observed.

"As we face some pedagogical challenges in the school I believe it is essential to have instructionally specific conversations with teachers so that together as a team we can better facilitate student and professional learning," said Rafia with great conviction.

"Well, the reason I am here today is because my daughter, Aisha, seems to have lost all interest in English. I'm very worried about her and am looking to you to help me because I trust you completely. You have always been honest with me and your sincerity is truly appreciated."

"Mariam, thank you for feeling comfortable in coming to me directly and I am truly sorry to hear that Aisha's interest in English seems to have diminished so much. I remember when she was in her earlier classes how passionate, creative and curious she was about English. Have you talked with Aisha about what's going on? And have you spoken with her grade 5 teacher?" Rafia asked calmly, always concerned about the human elements of leadership.

"I've tried but it seems Aisha's teacher follows a certain teaching "script" and is not really attuned to Aisha's learning and developmental needs."

Rafia was keen to be sure that the school was addressing Aisha's individual needs rather than marching through the many pages of the text book with little regard for student learning and achievement but she was also careful to be sure the teacher was given the voice and respect she deserved.

"How about I have a chat with her teacher and just try to find out a little bit more about Aisha's situation. After that I can get back to you to arrange a meeting with you and the teacher so that you can discuss Aisha's needs and arrange further meetings. I have an excellent relationship with Aisha's teacher and we have worked together before on some challenging pedagogical situations," Rafia suggested soothingly.

Mariam immediately felt a huge weight had been lifted from her shoulders as Rafia continued to reassure her and really listen to her concerns about her daughter's learning. Rafia was again offering some more tea and Mariam smiled as she passed her tea cup over for a refill.

They talked at length and Mariam decided she would look more deeply into Aisha's learner profile, her preferences for learning and find ways to work with Aisha's teachers to address her daughter's specific learning needs and interests.

"I think we all have knowledge that can contribute to and enhance the learning in our schools," said Rafia. "I've been reading recently about the special responsibilities of leadership within an Islamic educational system where the teacher is expected to be a guide to knowledge and to be a role model. We need to find ways for parents, teachers and students to take on increased opportunities for leadership roles and your being here is contributing to that. Thank you, Mariam.

Given that I see teachers as today's stewards for an invigorated profession and the number one means to improving children's learning I ask that our teachers here demonstrate a willingness to try new ideas to develop creativity, innovation, lifelong learning." Rafia smiled.

"This still seems to be a new concept for some," said Mariam.

"Still, I do think teacher leadership is continuing to emerge in pockets across the country and improve instruction and student achievement," Rafia reflected.

They chatted some more about the important parent-school partnerships necessary for greater parent and student engagement in UAE schools and when Um Aisha left Rafia's office she felt far more at ease and relaxed about the next steps for her daughter's education.

As the driver pulled up for Um Aisha, through my window I could see that she turned back and waved warmly at Rafia who had escorted her out. Her smile acknowledged that Rafia was a teacher leader, an innovator and change agent and that she always would be.

"Rafia Abbas clearly built her relationships on trust and transparency and she has always supported teachers and parent-school community relationships," I thought.

Rafia turned back into the school and smiled with satisfaction. I reflected on the fact that this was the work she really enjoyed doing – working with people, working with the educational community. She believed whole heartedly that this important work was what could change the nation. She had found many ways of serving her family and community throughout her career and she was widely recognized as an educational leader. Her multiple accomplishments are recognized formally and informally by those whose lives she has touched. Rafia Abbas has provided a broad range of service in the UAE to schooling and the local community particularly in the area of leadership for women. She is heavily invested in education, participating in TESOL Arabia and other Ministry of Education and Educational Zone committees; serving on work groups when needed; and, providing mentoring and coaching leadership as an advisor to the many teachers and students in UAE schools.

I then turned to the farewell speech I was drafting and reread it for the umpteenth time to check that it truly captured the essence of Rafia.

1.2   *The Farewell Speech*

Rafia Abbas has always attracted those around her. She is a pioneer and has been the first at many things. Rafia Abbas has always known that she can make a difference and has worked throughout her life to do so. She knows that the future of her country is in her hands and those of the teachers and educational leaders she works with. Rafia started out as a middle and high school teacher of English language in 1983. As her career progressed she became a supervisor of English teachers for the Dubai Educational Zone and then took on the role of Deputy Principal of a highly reputable private school in Dubai. No stranger to change and service to others, rather than adopt any one leadership style she adapted several with situational, participative and servant leadership resonating most with her leadership practices and perspectives.

She was the first person to win the Hamdan Award in 1998 for Distinctive Academic Performance as a distinguished supervisor. She felt royal and humble at the same time. When the award was announced and the door opened there were people all around Rafia. Lights flashed and the press followed her, in hot pursuit of an interview. Following Rafia all the way to the car, they asked her questions about how she felt to be the person honored for her exemplary performance and achievements in educational leadership. Rafia promised several interviews and smiled as the car pulled away from the crowd. This was a major achievement.

As a mother, Rafia Abbas constantly encouraged her children to excel. She encouraged the exact same excellence in her own classes. Rafia's professional knowledge and understanding extends far beyond her role as a teacher and Vice Principal. She has invested so actively in the professional relationships she develops and as a result she has shared a depth and wide range of professional knowledge about education, classroom pedagogy, and professional development with her colleagues. With Rafia Abbas all children learned and Rafia was one of the first learner-centered Emirati English teachers that children actually understood. Rafia Abbas was also one of the first teachers to change the way children were taught English language in the

UAE. Using an inclusive, engaging approach and hands on teaching strategies with real life examples of language she made English language learning fun and children were finally learning to communicate in English outside the classroom. She encouraged critical thinking and strived to foster independent lifelong learning in her learners. This was something extremely innovative and ground breaking in the early 1980s.

She was the first Ministry of Education supervisor to be a member of the international organization TESOL Inc. Again, she was honored with Rashida Badri for presenting a paper at the International TESOL Conference in Utah. She was the first to work with a team of colleagues asking government school principals to support a pilot project on cooperative learning, a methodology very close to Rafia's heart. Ever the innovator, risk taker, friend, visionary educative leader, through determination, a great sense of humor and a caring and principled communication approach, Rafia has impacted all those who know her and have worked with her.

Yes, I was satisfied with how the speech was shaping up. I continued to reflect on Rafia.

"As she plans to retire from the role of vice principal soon, I know she is looking forward to using her leadership knowledge and skills in her other complex life roles as mother, grandmother, wife and friend. She clearly celebrates the joys of motherhood and those of being a grandmother. Oh, the things she might do … the plans she has had made … and those plans she is making. I welcome Rafia's valuable leadership as a mentor to me in the coming years and I hope that I will continue to know Rafia Abbas for a very long time," I thought.

1.3   *Today*

Rafia is sitting in a coffee shop with her good friends still discussing the current state of play in education and schooling in the country.

"I thought it when I was a teacher, a supervisor and Deputy Principal and I still think it now … the future of our country is in our hands, the hands of its teachers. We must find ways to love and nurture our children so that they realize their true potential and become the best that they can be – empowered, responsible, capable," Rafia shared animatedly.

Rashida nodded in agreement, "So true, Abbas."

Rafia continued, "I am reading His Highness Sheikh Mohammad Bin Rashid Al Maktoum, Vice President and Prime Minister of the UAE and Ruler of Dubai's *Flashes of Thought* and there is a quote of his that I believe captures the essence of it perfectly: "The progress of countries, peoples and civilization starts with education. The future of nations starts in their schools" (p. 74).

"If we don't teach our children, who will?" Rafia let the question hang in the air as her friends answered in silent unison:

"Exactly, Rafia, exactly. Emiratis must take the future into their own hands, seize opportunities that come their way and rise to the challenges of the times. In the words of H.H. Sheikh Mohammad "we should get accustomed to not getting accustomed." "

CHAPTER 7

Rashida Badri

I don't believe in 'I' as much as I believe in 'we.'

∴

Rashida's legacy is to have worked 'shoulder to shoulder' with a generation of educators, bringing out the best in them and allowing them to grow and develop as leaders to achieve more than they realized they could. Rashida Badri is the CEO at Greenwood International School in Dubai in the United Arab Emirates (UAE). Greenwood International School is an American curriculum school and was founded in 2006 under the leadership of Rashida Badri who until recently served as its principal. Rashida graduated from the United Arab Emirates University in 1982 with a Bachelor of Education degree in English Literature.

Rashida began her teaching career in a secondary school teaching English. After 10 years as a teacher she moved into the role of Supervisor for the Ministry of Education. In this role she was an active member of TESOL Arabia and Rashida encouraged her colleagues to attend the TESOL Arabia Conferences held annually in the UAE. She was a key player in the first English Education Conference held at Zayed University in 1998. This Conference was a huge success and teachers came from all over the UAE to attend. In 2000 Rashida became Head of Department of Education Affairs for the Dubai Zone. She was responsible for all public schools, Zone supervisors, principals, teacher, students and adult education in Dubai. In 2003 Rashida took up a role as Assistant Director for Private Education providing leadership for over 125 private schools, 10 curricula and 105 000 students. In 2006 she was again drawn back to leading learning at Greenwood International School where she has provided exemplary leadership in support of the whole child and improving student achievement and their success. The school roll has expanded dramatically in the last decade resulting in a major extension to its buildings.

1   Rashida's Story

"Rashida, quickly baba, it's time to go," said her father. "Your cousins are waiting for you in the car."

It's their weekly trip to see an English movie. They all loved the movies and couldn't wait to be sitting in the cool dark theatre with all those wonderful English words and sounds floating through the air.

Rashida smiled and rushed to the car. She was probably the one who loved this experience the most of all. She had a real passion for the English language and language learning in general. In fact, Rashida had started taking English lessons from the Indian lady next door when she was just eight years old. She couldn't wait to meet her teacher each afternoon. Those two hours each day were like entering into another magic place for Rashida and during those years learning with her teacher, watching her father talk to foreigners and constantly trying to read their lips she became completely enamored with the English language.

"One day I want to be like that," she thought. From that point on she knew that to be an English teacher was her goal.

2   Facing up to the Challenges

It was 1982 and when Rashida finished her degree within the month she had begun teaching in a secondary school. It was 25 March. Excited and nervous, on her first day she was asked to teach grade 11. This was the beginning of many challenging situations for Rashida as an educator and teacher leader.

Some weeks later in the staff room, Rashida was reflecting on those experiences of the first days. She remembered a conversation with Alfra and felt as if she were right there back in the same classroom.

"When they stand up there I am in front of a wall of very tall girls. They appeared huge to me. It's terrifying. I mean some are older than me!" Rashida said.

"I know I have to deal with it and I will but I'm sure it will be challenging. I can see that I don't have much practical teaching experience as my degree is largely theoretical."

"Well, Rashida, just so you know, I still feel so unsupported myself," said Afra.

"I mean so much more needs to happen in terms of helping us change our teaching, you know, move away from the 'chalk and talk.' Yes, we have our supervisors but we need more from them than what they can offer. I don't want 'fault finders.' I want a helper to take my hand and show me – talking is not like seeing," said Afra.

"Mmm ... it seems that the system merely requires supervisors to monitor the theoretical side. But this is not enough for a novice like me. I am looking for new ideas and new ways of doing things. I feel that we need to be able to visit model teachers and talk with them. Some teachers who are doing excellent work could be great mentors and colleagues" said Rashida.

"I completely agree," said Afra. "It would make such a difference to be able to work together."

"If I ever become a Supervisor I really want to change that when I start the job," Rashida thought.

3   **The Golden Days**

Having completed her Bachelor of Education Degree Rashida eagerly embraced her English teaching job in a government secondary school. However, it wasn't until she became a Supervisor of English that she really had the chance to excel and develop her leadership.

Rashida was unexpectedly very attracted to the idea of Supervision. The number of local teachers new to the profession was increasing and Rashida was determined to work at changing the focus on individuality within schools and instead foster a climate of collegiality, collectivity and communication. She also knew there would be challenges. Many of the teachers she would be supervising had taught her at school.

Animatedly she talked through some of her ideas with another like-minded Supervisor.

Rashida spoke with conviction. "You see I believe leadership and administration are completely different. Administration is only paperwork. When you provide educational leadership for teachers you are building their personalities," she said. "Their learning in turn affects the students – you are dealing with character building at all levels."

"You know, even before I started in this role I was thinking "what can I offer the teachers and other supervisors who are my colleagues?" I have had many ideas about possible learning opportunities for teachers. I mean, why don't we introduce peer observations? Teachers could visit each other's classes, move from school to school to observe good teaching? That may help alleviate some of the fear to talk openly about the challenges we face," Rashida suggested.

"These are wonderful ideas. I also feel the need to do more as well," Reem said.

Rashida paused and took a sip of water. "Yes and it is such sensitive work."

Visiting schools to identify areas for improvement and then somehow getting the principals to make positive changes is challenging."

"I completely agree," said Reem.

For Rashida, ensuring best practice in the schools was particularly important especially when the practices could be deemed harmful to children. For her it was also all about how she managed her social interactions.

Rashida went on "I think it is your personality that is important – it is essential to deal with people as colleagues and then you can influence change. My aim is to find out what is happening in the schools and I try to do this by visiting them often. That way I am not merely "talking from the office."

Taking another sip Rashida paused again and looked pensive.

"I think because university is so theoretical teachers and supervisors continue to struggle to develop practical skills."

"Yes, I know that pre-service teachers don't observe classes," Reem said.

"That's right and there is no practice teaching or internship program either. The system seems to force teachers and supervisors to focus on the theoretical side."

"Teachers new to the profession need more support and mentoring, right?" commented Reem.

"Well, this is the floor and we have to stand on it." Rashida smiled. "We need to see model teachers teach. So many of my colleagues long to visit good classes and talk with the teachers so that we can learn from their experience in the classroom and in the school. I want to make this happen in my job as a Supervisor," Rashida said passionately.

"Me too," said Reem, equally as committed.

"How about we start doing some workshops and seminars?" Yes, and why don't we organize an English Conference. It would be a first for the UAE and I'm sure we would get a lot of interest from teachers." Rashida suggested.

Rashida was a key player in the first English Conference held at Zayed University in 1998. This Conference was a huge success and teachers came from all over the UAE to attend. As a Supervisor and active member of TESOL Arabia Rashida encouraged her colleagues to attend the TESOL Arabia Conferences initially held annually in Al Ain then later in Dubai. Teachers loved the TESOL Arabia initiatives, her own personal professional learning initiatives and the demand for more of the same continued to grow over the years.

During her time as Supervisor Rashida focused on developing her own knowledge and skills. She attended workshops, seminars and undertook training always with the intention of sharing her learnings with others. With a team of like minded colleagues Rashida designed and delivered professional development programs for teachers.

When Rashida visited those classes she realized the impact these professional development sessions were having by observing how instruction had changed for the better. Teachers were really benefiting. It was then that she decided to encourage them to become teacher trainers themselves. She also encouraged teachers to welcome colleagues into their classrooms. These colleagues came from within their own schools and beyond.

Rashida reflected back on those times and thought about the Director of the Zone at that time. He had had such an influence on her as he was very supportive of the Supervisors, demanded excellent work from them, maintained high expectations and rewarded them with untold opportunities to learn professionally and personally.

"That man had a huge affect on me personally and professionally. He helped me build and develop my personality and identity. I guess he showed me how it was possible to develop leadership in others and so that is what I tried to do as well," she thought.

Rashida was concerned with both the individual and collective learning of English teachers. When she conducted walk throughs in the schools, however, she did not single out individuals. At those times she was concerned with the well being of all and whatever she had to give she willingly shared with everybody. Nevertheless, there were times when her focus turned to the individuals. Whilst there were teachers who contented themselves with earning their monthly salaries, there were others who strove to do more, to make a difference and to excel in their teaching. Rashida was always overjoyed when she could identify such teachers. Rashida identified flexibility, willingness to learn and confidence in these women. These teachers were clearly leaders in their schools and their leadership skills and dispositions convinced her that they could make a difference beyond their own classrooms and schools. Rashida felt strongly that they deserved somebody to support and back them and so this is exactly what she did.

In professional development sessions for the English teachers she not only aimed to develop their knowledge of current methods and instructional practices, she also worked on their character development by deliberately encouraging them to help other subject area teachers. She set high standards and gave them the responsibility to complete their work without interference. As a result today so many more women are in educational leadership positions as a result of Rashida's modeling shared leadership, mentoring, coaching, support and faith in their ability to do well. Today she is still involved, encouraging them to do more, to strive to reach their full potential.

4   Head of Department, Dubai Zone

Ten years later Rashida took her next step in her leadership journey and moved from English Supervisor to Ministry of Education administrator.

In the office of a Senior Director, Rashida and the Senior Director were engaged in serious conversation. The Senior Director smiled and said "Rashida, we need someone like you in the Zone. Would you consider making the transition from supervision to administration?"

"Rashida, I know that you value your colleagues like friends and sisters. It is clear to me that you believe in nurturing their strengths and supporting them so that they become increasingly confident and sure of themselves in the classroom," said the Senior Director.

"What has been particularly effective in your supervision is that you have visited schools and handled important and sensitive matters with professionalism and good grace. You have had several hundred teachers reporting to you over these ten years and your team has had great success in making gradual moves towards positive and effective change in schools," the Senior Director continued.

"Thank you. Yes, it was a really wonderful time," Rashida said fondly. "Those were my golden days for sure. I mean, typically supervisors were not popular with the teachers. The job had a bad reputation because of the personality of some supervisors who took the position to mean fault finder. However, I started with the positives then mentioned a couple of areas that teachers could focus on for improvement. I had a feeling that rewarding with genuine praise would foster better communication. I made a point of taking colleagues by the hand and praising them in front of their peers and supervisors. The relationships we developed are still alive and well today. We were not supervisors managing teachers anymore. We were colleagues sharing the leadership, engaging in action research together for the benefit of student learning. I have a hands on approach to supervision. I have never wanted to talk from the office. The point of my leadership is to develop the person and foster life long learning," said Rashida.

"And so teacher development has been my first and primary focus. For me, I could have easily demanded the teachers attend workshops and so on but I just couldn't do it. I wanted to bring out their personalities. I wanted to build their confidence, enrich the work itself. I have been extremely lucky. My colleagues were always ready to help, for example at conferences. We are called the 'gang,' 'Rashida's gang'– people called us to organize conferences. I guess you could say that my leadership is to build people, give them responsibility and give them the means to do a good job."

"So would you consider making the transition?" the Senior Director of the Zone asked again.

"I must say I am truly honored. Fostering leadership potential has been very important for me. I can't say that I have not mentored possible candidates to replace me should I move to another position. In fact there are two young women whom I have been working particularly closely with, grooming them to take over if need be. It's just so much a part of my nature to be working closely with my 'sisters' to improve schooling, teaching and learning," she said. Still Rashida was not sure about such a move.

And yet she did leave supervision and started something completely different – administration of schools in general. She wasn't really even clear how it all came to be. What was that something in her that seeks change? It grabbed hold of her and she plunged right in again.

Sitting and chatting with a colleague one day Rashida was asked to explain more about her role as Head of Department.

"So your brief was to 'handle pretty much everything' it seems," commented Hessa. "I mean, obviously everything had to go through you Rashida and then it was sent to the director of the Zone.

"Yes, I was part of the senior team of three and then of course there was the Director, himself. As Head of Department of Education Affairs, Dubai Zone I was in charge of all public schools, Zone supervisors, principals, teachers, students and adult education," Rashida said.

Hessa's eyes almost popped out of her head. "So what does that mean?"

"Well, it means I had to supervise everything related to schools from A to Z. I even had to supervise school security. My main responsibilities though were student registration, teacher appointments, teacher transfers and all student examinations from grade one to grade eleven," Rashida explained.

Hessa couldn't stop herself and jumped in to comment "But doing all that must have been a nightmare!"

Rashida smiled as she remembered those extremely challenging times. She had struggled with the transition initially and found administrative work very different and extremely challenging. After 10 years focusing on teacher and student learning all of a sudden she was dealing with schools, buildings, teachers, student workshops, parents and other members of the community. It became a day and night job for three full years. Just as she had in her supervisory position, not only was she responsible for K-12 schooling but she also dealt with adult education classes from 5–8 pm in the evenings [this was done both as a supervisor and administrator]. Her most time consuming and challenging job was the distribution of teachers in schools because it was impossible to satisfy everybody. However, drawing on her excellent interpersonal skills and her strong relationships with school administrators as a result of her work as a supervisor, she was able to persuade the majority of school leaders to accept teacher placement decisions.

Rising to each challenge was part of Rashida's character and yet she longed to be back working closely with her first passion and the subject that drew her to education in the first place – English. Having fought from childhood to become an English teacher, not hearing, speaking and living the language everyday was very difficult for Rashida. Returning to supervision was not permitted and gradually the absence of English in Rashida's daily life shifted to feelings of overwhelming loss– she was tortured. By sheer luck a new position came up as Assistant Director for Private Education. The Ministry needed a bilingual person and Rashida, recognizing the great opportunity for what it was, made the decision to change positions.

5   Assistant Director for Private Education

"I had full authority to enter and provide leadership for 150 schools and I really wanted to make the new position work," said Rashida.

"You must have met such a wide variety of people in the role?" said Hessa.

"Yes, it was very interesting for me. In this new role I had to deal with nationalities from everywhere. I was responsible for 10 curriculums, 105 000 students, 125 schools, and 8500 teachers and administrators. I had to find out the necessary curriculum information ranging from Russian to French to Tagalog. My work life was like a 'global village. I really loved that job.

Later on in the year at the Hamdan Awards celebration Hessa was with Shaima, an English supervisor, and Asma, a local English teacher who had received an award. They were chatting together as they waited for some other friends.

"Mabrook Asma," exclaimed Hessa. She was then called away to talk to some other colleagues.

"Yes Mabrook Asma. I am so proud of you," said Shaima." "This is your *second* award. You must be feeling very proud too."

"Yes, I am really happy about it. But you know it's at times like this that I think about others who believed in me and started me on the journey to where I am now."

The two women looked at each other and smiled. "You're thinking of Rashida Badri, aren't you?"

"Yes. She was amazing – kind of charismatic really. I remember her kindness towards us teachers particularly when she had the responsibility for the transfer of teachers among schools. That's the kind of position where everyone comes to you and 'fights' about the decisions, but Rashida had the ability to stand her ground in an open understanding way – people just 'cooled down' with her. She had a way of letting you make the choices that were best rather than trying to control you or the choices you may made."

Shaima smiled in agreement. "What I remember about Rashida is her kind, calm and soothing manner and the fact that she gained the respect of all those that work with her.

I recall the way she could 'lift' and encourage teachers. I remember when I was a teaching English at a local school I prepared some practice books for the secondary classes. When Rashida saw them she said 'these are extraordinary. You should take these beyond the school.' She really encouraged me and then I distributed the books to other schools and got a good reputation and praise. She kept on encouraging me to become a supervisor and you know what – I won 'best supervisor' last year. It was all because of her. She has a magic influence."

"I know exactly what you mean," laughed Asma. "There was a time earlier in my career when I was transferred to a new school and I just wanted to resign. I was very upset and emotional and Rashida patiently sat and listened to me so kindly. Then she unexpectedly 'stopped me in my tracks' when she said 'think about what you are saying' in a tone that was really quite strict and firm. It *did* make me think, and when she saw I was okay she went back to her more gentle approach. She was able to get me back to my old school, Alhamdulillah, and look where I am now! I am no longer shy and instead am confident and believe in myself because of Rashida's influence."

"Rashida has always been a leader. When you follow her you know you're safe. She really cares for and protects people in her team," added Shaima. "Her leadership is people oriented. She really touches people with her humanity, principles, support and guidance. She manages to inspire people to make the right choices. I can see she is regarded by so many as a mother to them."

"I think what is also impressive about her is her professional expertise. You know how some people are all about 'show,' but Rashida only ever presents effective ideas she knows will make a difference and that you can use immediately in your classroom" enthused Asma. "She's had such an impact on the professionalism and knowledge of the teachers she's worked with. When I look at English teachers and Supervisors in the UAE, so many of them have developed leadership skills because of Rashida's support and encouragement."

"And now she's doing such a wonderful job as principal of Greenwood school," commented Shaima. It's interesting how she's sort of come full circle from having a direct impact on kids in the classroom, to helping other teachers lead effective learning, and back to a direct impact on the kids in her school. What a truly exceptional woman, friend and colleague she is!"

6   Greenwood School, Dubai

Buthina was working quietly in her office just when she saw Rashida hurry past her to greet Sheikha Abdullah. She reflected on the ever increasing success of Greenwood, her own daughter's happiness and learning there and on how happy she was working there with Rashida, her best friend and other mother.

Buthina remembered how as a child no matter how busy Rashida was with work and other important matters she had given Buthina her undivided attention.

"She really listened to me and took me seriously no matter what my age was," she thought.

She continued to reflect on the enormous impact Rashida had had on her life. Rashida continued to teach her and take care of her and here she was doing this with her vast staff and student body. The quality of education at Greenwood is well known throughout the community. Because of her reputation and her track record in education Rashida has been able to build and develop a nearly perfect school. She considers people's issues and so people feel that they are going to their second home when they head for the school. The teachers, parents, staff and students are her wider family and she is well loved for her leadership of the school. Rashida is firm but friendly and she has lived these words throughout her leadership practices and career. Buthina knew that from the first years that Rashida began teaching, some 30 years ago, she had had to find a way to be firm in class to gain the respect of the grade 11 and 12 students who were older than her. She also had a kind and caring way with the students outside of class that enabled her to develop trusting relationships. She had the ability to initiate improvements and change in the curriculum working with teachers who were at least ten years older than her by gaining their respect of her innovations and leadership practices. As the years have passed, Rashida has continued to gain respect and trust in the community. It is clear that she takes time to get to know all the people with whom she works and she has uncanny intuition about what people are thinking and feeling. It's as if she can see into their minds. She uses this incredible ability to determine how best to work and deal with each and every person. She is like a sister to some of them, an auntie to others and a mother to me.

Buthina looked up as a parent knocked on her office door. She was transported back to the busy work day at the highly regarded Greenwood School and she smiled.

CHAPTER 8

Fatma Al Marri

Leadership development is like a circle that grows. The more senior you become, the more you learn and develop as a leader through experience and practice.

∴

Fatma's legacy is her key role in the development of women's leadership in the UAE and her significant impact on the quality of the private school sector in Dubai, leading innovation and change through the promotion of Emirati national identity, enhanced student achievement and parent and community confidence in the excellence of their children's schools.

Fatma Al Marri is currently the CEO of the Dubai School Agency of the Knowledge and Human Development Authority, with responsibility for policy development and leading innovation in the private school sector. She honed her early leadership skills as a teacher and principal in Dubai. From 2007–2011, she was one of nine women who were inaugural members of the Federal National Council (FNC), contributing advice to the UAE government on social and educational issues. Since 2010, Fatma has also contributed to the wider community context through membership of the Board of Trustees of Hamdan e-University, the Dubai Government Traffic Safety Committee and the Dubai Appreciation Award for Community Services Committee. She is also a member of the Board of Trustees of the Higher Colleges of Technology.

1   Fatma's Story

Um Shamma had just put down her phone. Her hands were ever so slightly trembling and she was barely smiling. She continued eating her meal as both her daughter and sister looked at her quizzically. Having still not broken her silence, her daughter, Shamma, asked "Who was that Umi?" But she couldn't say. She had been sworn to secrecy. She finished her meal and then calmly and quickly excused herself from the table.

"I'll never forget this moment, never," Um Shamma thought with such a range of extreme emotions. "I've made it. Finally, the day has come where all my hard

© KONINKLIJKE BRILL NV, LEIDEN, 2018 | DOI 10.1163/9789004372948_008

work and effort has paid off. I am recognized and appreciated by the community for what I have done and how much I have given to education in the UAE."

Fatma Al Marri had just been called by the Sheikh's office and informed that she had been shortlisted as a member of the Federal National Council (FNC). Several people had suggested that she put herself forward and they would vote for her but she had refused. As it turned out she had been put forward by the Sheikh's office. It was only the next day that her family found out that such an honor had been bestowed upon their mother, sister and daughter.

That morning Fatma got up, read the paper and paused at times to reflect on the many different lived leadership experiences she had had during her life up to that point. She was being interviewed by Rania Omar from Dubai One and thought she should go over the questions again in her head in preparation. She had never liked to refer to notes but wanted to be sure she was sufficiently prepared for the high profile interview. She put down the newspaper and turned to the questions before her. As she read them her mind wandered ever so slightly and she found herself reflecting on how she had gotten to this point. What had been recognized by others to result in this great honor? Just then the doorbell rang. As Fatma came into the entry hall she saw that Rania, the reporter and her crew had arrived. Fatma gave them all a warm smile and ushered them into the home's majlis where she had formal meetings with guests. After much preparation, lighting and sound checking Um Shamma found herself sitting opposite Rania addressing a range of questions that so many wanted to hear the answers to.

You were born the eldest daughter among six brothers and five sisters. How did this impact your leadership development?" Rania probed.

"Well, I guess you could say my leadership potential was evident and developed during my childhood years," Fatma responded. My sense of responsibility developed very early as I helped my mother take care of my siblings. My late father was a Nokhada, a leader, a great man and an important role model in my life. He worked very hard and I loved to listen to and learn from the stories about his travels," Fatma recalled wistfully.

"And what about your education and its influence on you?" Rania asked.

"I enjoyed school from the very outset and it was during my schooling that I was influenced by some excellent teachers who encouraged me and developed my confidence in my own abilities. Teachers continually gave me responsibilities to foster my independence and activities to develop my potential," Fatma said. "I remember at school I also initiated a variety of leadership roles for myself including gathering girls together in order to teach them. I was the organizer."

"How did this shape your leadership development and also your work as an English teacher?" Rania encouraged.

"Yes, these personal leadership experiences significantly influenced my leadership style and practices at work. When I became an English teacher in a secondary school I found myself working as part of a team with my previous teacher, Raja Al Gurg, as the principal. Immediately she gave me responsibilities that I initially thought I may not be able to manage! But she trusted me to do my best and naturally I did. You know, I learned much about effective leadership from her ...." Fatma's voice trailed off as the director said "Cut."

As they took coffee and dates, Rania asked Fatma some more biographical information about her career in preparation for the next stage of the interview.

"I taught for six years and then took on the role of vice-principal for two years before becoming principal at a preparatory school for three years and I was always keen to understand the students' needs and interests. By getting to know them I was better able to lead the teaching team towards improved student outcomes. I then took a position as principal of Al-Raya Girls' School for Secondary Education and remained there for over ten years," Fatma explained.

After another round of makeup and sound checking, Rania asked Fatma to define what leadership meant for her.

"Leadership, for me, then and now, is how a person is capable of influencing other people. It's about bringing people together to achieve a shared goal and to solve problems together even if they are personal problems. You know, since I was a small girl I dreamed that I would be able to try and make a difference for my country and now I am living it," Fatma said passionately.

"As a principal I remember thinking something has to be done and now I am here to do it. It takes a lot of work and effort and it's the working with people that for me is the most critical skill. And it's the feeling that I am doing something and that I am not alone. There is a passion that you feel when everybody is working together to make the dream come true. It's this passion that is my most effective tool.

"And then there was the move from the operations level to the strategy and policy level," Rania probed. "It seems that the move from high school principal to CEO of the School Agency (SA) (an agency under the Knowledge and Human Development Authority) was a significant change for others to grasp."

"Yes, the School Agency was established to oversee the development and management of school based educational services in Dubai. It was a challenge at first as some people were not sure if I had the skills to do the job."

"Still despite several setbacks, and some unkindness at times, you remained determined to carry on and reach the goals you had established with your team. I see that understanding, appreciation and tolerance are some of the attributes that you draw on to develop relationships," Rania observed.

"Yes, these are critical to gain buy in and develop a shared vision. Yes, the move to the School Agency was a big change. I continually ask 'How can we better prepare our children for the future?' Children are changing rapidly as a result of global challenges. Where are we taking our children? We are afraid if we do X then Y will happen. We need to set goals, take risks, be courageous and give our children alternatives. We need to increase the quality of public and private education to meet community needs," Fatma said emphatically.

Fatma continued, "You see, in my opinion there is a gap between those in education and the families that the education system aims to serve and support. I believe education begins at home and yet others do not see it this way. I am constantly trying to manage others' expectations of the education system. People in the community are still not clear about what they want for their children – is it Arabic? English? Leadership? Knowledge? Critical thinking?

"So how do you find a way to balance the competing priorities you have?" Rania asked.

"I continue to try to balance my life and prioritize what is important. Most people have no idea how busy I am and the sacrifices such work demands. But each year is better than the last. KHDA is gaining greater acceptance in the schools and to keep this up we try to involve the schools in everything we do. I often get asked what advice I have for the younger generations, particularly young Emirati women. All I can say is have something that you believe in doing and then just keep on working toward your dream. I hold true to my goals, remain focused and ambitious. I found a way to do what I wanted to do within the family and proved to others that I am capable of doing what I do. Self confidence and effective communication skills are so important. I guess I developed my own confidence as I experienced different challenges and situations. When I fail I try to learn from the mistakes I make. Working collaboratively with others is also a way to develop yourself. I have worked in several different environments. These varied experiences also develop confidence, because you have to be able to present your opinions, negotiate with and persuade others," Fatma noted.

"You've also done some voluntary work in the community haven't you?" Rania asked. Fatma nodded.

"Such diverse experience demands dealing with different people in different ways I'd expect. Can you talk more about the importance of communication in this context?" Rania asked.

"I have had to be able to present my point of view in a variety of contexts. I need to communicate appropriately and respectfully, listen to others' views and argue and defend my own opinions, values and beliefs," Fatma said.

"I often hear that some Emirati women struggle with presenting and persuading their families to allow them to follow their dreams?" Rania asked.

"Yes, sure. Each individual has to deal with different circumstances. I try to suggest that these young women find out the reasons why a family member may not want them to take a certain pathway and then try to change it in an appropriate way. I think the skill of negotiating and persuading is essential. More families let their daughters travel overseas, drive, and work with men. Nowadays men and women work together more and women are able to work anywhere not just in education. Women in the UAE are in a good situation compared to other countries in the region. We shouldn't forget that the UAE is a very young country that has developed extremely quickly compared to most other countries in the world. Rapid progress has been made but not necessarily in all spheres. Perhaps the community culture has not developed at the same rapid pace as the economy."

"For example?" Rania prompted.

"Well, we have only just started to develop women's leadership in the public sphere and to create a shared vision for women's leadership in the UAE. In my role as CEO of the School Agency I try to encourage more responsibility for women at KHDA, in the schools and in the classes. Young children should be given opportunities to take on greater responsibility in the home and at school.

Responsibility should be built in at various levels of the curriculum and built upon. If we want to build leadership capacity amongst our students then opportunities to practice leadership need to be provided in the educational system. Leadership has to be practical, not only something we read about in books. We lack this in our UAE educational programs. When a child speaks to you the skills of leadership can be identified almost at once – eye contact, confidence, ability to communicate main ideas. I see more of these skills in children from private schools than those in our public government funded schools," Fatma said.

Fatma heard her daughter come into the room and she looked up. Shamma smiled at her mother who smiled back at her daughter.

For a while Um Shamma was lost in thought as she remembered those earlier years when she was struggling as a single parent to raise her daughter and manage her own job and family. This made her more courageous, she thought.

Having married in her early twenties, it was at that point that her most challenging and her most satisfying leadership experiences occurred. Having lost her husband after eighteen months of marriage she found herself alone with the responsibility of a two month old baby. She moved back to the family home and found herself helping with responsibilities for her brothers and sisters as well as her own daughter. As the eldest she wanted to take on this leadership role for the family when she returned to the house.

She believed these early challenges significantly shaped her personality and made her into a leader. As her leadership roles changed Fatma gained invaluable leadership experience. As a teacher leader Fatma aimed to foster genuine caring relationships with her students and to be there as a role model for them. When she transitioned to vice principal, more often than not, she found herself managing day to day school operations and having to deal with even more people – students, parents, teachers, Ministry staff. In contrast, later as a school principal she needed to use her role to influence people to change things rather than enforce regulations. Her fundamental core belief at that time was the importance of the teachers. Her focus on the teachers, children and parents was the key to effective change in the school.

Well aware of many of her strengths and weaknesses, it was Fatma's own daughter who was best able to make explicit the weaknesses that others would not dare tell her about. She truly valued her daughter's honesty and support. She recalled Shamma's reminders of her tendency at times to become too involved in the issues that she was dealing with.

Rania asked Shamma, "Will you be able to join us for a while, Shamma?"

"Sure," said Shamma.

"How would you describe your mother's leadership, Shamma?" Rania began.

"Well, to me, Mum is a charismatic type of leader. She is loved by her teams and she loves them. She adapts her approach to the needs of the situation and she also takes a transformational perspective. For my mother, having a clear vision and purpose is very important. She believes that a vision should be created collaboratively so that it is shared and owned by everyone. She believes that this establishes a sense of individual and collective commitment, and a sense of belonging."

"Yes, that's right," Fatma agreed. "I think people are more committed to achieving goals if they are shared and grounded in a collective vision."

"Is this what you aimed to do when you were a school principal?" Rania asked.

"Yes, absolutely," Fatma said with conviction. "We shared a collective commitment to the moral purpose of education. The community recognized the good work we were doing in the school. We had a long waiting list of students who wanted to attend the school. We had a very good teacher retention rate – teachers simply did not want to leave the school."

"What about at the School Agency?" Rania asked.

"Well, in this role my work expanded from being responsible for one school to being responsible for over 150 private schools and early learning centres in the Emirate, with more than 225,000 students and over 15 different curricula and with a variety of approaches."

"Again everyone participated as we created the blueprint for the School Agency. I worked on establishing effective relationships through open channels of communication as colleagues at the School Agency solved problems and made decisions together," Fatma said.

"My mother is authentic and natural. She is a simple person and people trust her because she is genuine," Shamma smiled. "She appreciates the people she works with for their qualities, not only as employees but also as human beings. Her openness and spontaneity make people trust her and confide in her. She is trusted because she takes time to get to know people and so people are attracted to my mother. She sits with them and they talk about issues and their lives. She genuinely cares about their ideas and concerns. She seizes the opportunities that exist to get to know other people better. She is also passionate about what she believes in and this inspires respect and motivates others. She is consistent and she keeps her promises which makes people feel safe and supported, and yet she is still able to be firm when the situation calls for it. I think she is so successful because she is able to maintain such a balance," Shamma said. "Not only with women or Arabs but with everyone. As a child I was amazed when I saw her talking with foreigners. She seemed so natural and so at ease. She's spontaneous. She inspires me. Just as she is a role model to others, she is a role model to me. My mother has such personal courage and strength. She was a single parent at a very young age. In fact she was responsible for her whole family at an early age. This was a huge, emotional and physical challenge for my Mum but she was already a very strong and responsible person.

A lot of people would probably suggest that Mum was very lenient with me but in fact she was firm. She had a vision for herself and for me and she was determined that we would get there. Having said that, she was and is very open to ideas and has never been extremist in her views. She does not see things as black or white and she can change her mind about an idea or situation as a result. She had very high expectations of me and she always said "Do your best, give it 100%, participate in competitions, aim for the highest grades ..." that was my Mum's way. And we could talk together about anything really. She had such faith in me and believed that I could reach these high standards. Her positive energy and the positive messages she gave me have made me who I am today. She could have been extremely overprotective of me given the circumstances. Yet, she was firm and I was disciplined but at the same time she didn't stop me from doing things.

"Can you give me some examples?" Rania asked.

"Well, there was a ski trip when I was at school and a lot of the girls were not allowed to go but my mother said I could. She also approved of me getting my driver's license when I was twenty one and wanted me to take responsibility for myself very early on. It took a lot of courage and discipline to trust me with such responsibility. Similarly to me, she believes in developing leadership in others and sees this as an important role of an effective leader – the creation of new leaders. She didn't make decisions for me; she let me make my own decisions and choices at a very young age. If Mum hadn't allowed me certain freedoms I don't think I would have developed my own leadership skills and practices when I was younger."

"How do you develop leadership in others?" Rania asked turning to Fatma.

"Well, I delegate," Fatma smiled. "I give people autonomy, responsibility and freedom to make decisions, while at the same time supervising their progress so that they are accountable for their decisions and actions. To me, this is essential training for those who will become future leaders."

"You were finally recognized for all the good you were doing to find solutions for the challenges faced by schools when you were appointed Head of the School Agency," Rania said.

"I guess, you could say that, although I see it more as a passion. A life mission. Effective education empowers the youth and provides the freedom to think independently. As a parent, teacher, principal and now Head of the School Agency, I have constantly worked to push boundaries to improve the school system. It has not been easy because people often do not like change and prefer to stay in their own comfort zones," Fatma emphasized.

"One month after becoming the CEO of the School Agency, you were appointed as a member of the FNC. That appointment clearly indicates how respected you are as a leader," Rania commented.

"It took more than twenty years of hard work, effort, perseverance and courage to reach this position," said Fatma. "I have advocated for women's empowerment throughout my career and I feel proud of the changes that have happened during my lifetime. I am so very proud of my daughter and proud of the young women who are graduating from universities across the UAE," Fatma said.

"We, too, are proud of all that you have achieved Fatma Al Marri. Thank you and Shamma for your time here today," said Rania concluding the interview.

Um Shamma smiled. She again recalled that call from the Sheikh's office. It was much later that the enormity of the responsibility of her new role in the

FNC and the task at hand really hit her, so much so, that she couldn't eat for the rest of the day. Another chapter was beginning in her leadership learning journey. She reflected again on her own leadership philosophy:

> *Leadership development is like a circle that grows. The more senior you become, the more you learn and develop as a leader through experience and practice.*

CHAPTER 9

Family, Realizing Potential and Relationships

The basis of strong family relationships is caring and commitment. In order to realize your full potential, it is essential that you know and live according to your core values. These are the things that shape how you view yourself, others, and the world around you. The key to developing relationships includes making relationships a priority, communicating effectively and providing support for each other.

∴

In our analysis of the women's stories three significant themes emerged. The first of these was the critical significance of parental and/or family encouragement and support of these women from very early on in their lives. Although the number of participants is small their stories provide examples that appear to counter the Euro-centric metanarrative around leadership capacity and opportunities for women compared to men in Emirati society. The second key theme was how the women worked towards their essential purpose of realizing their own leadership potential and that of others. Building and sustaining relationships was the third key theme in this study. The women's stories consistently highlight the use of relational leadership practices. Underpinning these three key findings was the significance of their own values which emerged from Islam within the family context; were nurtured through the process of realizing their own potential and that of others and consistently implemented in their relational leadership practices.

When analyzing the five stories, a conceptual framework emerged from the data. The framework for analysis of the individual stories of the five women is underpinned by the view that they each had an understanding and knowledge of self that went beyond the self to interconnectedness with others built upon a strong sense of vision and purpose and underpinned by a depth of knowledge and wisdom accumulated over time and it is those elements that determined their leadership practices. This perspective assumes that leaders' dispositions go beyond the ego and are concerned with positive (Cameron, 2008) and authentic leadership (Luthans & Avolio, 2003). We saw consistent evidence of the role of self in context and the significant influences of family, community, culture, society and intergenerational elements. They acknowledged the value of all people and their leadership held at its core the realization of human potential including that of themselves. The second factor is how they worked to achieve that vision and purpose, initiating and seizing leadership opportunities that presented themselves.

1   Family Relationships and Encouragement

The thematic analysis of the unique individual stories identified several common values which emerged from their own lived experiences in the context of family, society and Islam. The five participants' leadership practices built on solid foundations and beliefs where authenticity was a key characteristic of their leadership (Luthans & Avolio, 2003). When considering the leadership work of the five women within their family and cultural context it was evident that this reflected their individual and collective values, beliefs and practices. Shah (2006) highlights how in an Islamic culture knowledge and learning have significant stature. Educational leadership in this context involves teaching with knowledge and understanding, guiding with wisdom and values, and caring with responsibility and commitment (Shah, 2006). These three dimensions are evident in the stories of each of our participants.

What became apparent early on in the analysis was the significant impact of family relationships in the development of particular values in the women such as courage, humility, strength, responsibility, honesty, reliability, sincerity and dedication. It was clear that who these women were was very strongly centred in their Islamic faith, where they had come from and in almost every case how their fathers and/or mothers had encouraged and supported them to realize their potential (Avolio & Gardner, 2005).

Fatma, Rashida and Raja for example were strongly influenced by their fathers' encouragement and support for their further education and career development. In Raja's case her father himself held a significant leadership position in the service of the UAE and was a key role model in the development of her own leadership practices of thorough preparation, punctuality, self discipline and measured decision making. The influence of their mother was also mentioned by Raya, Fatma and Raja in relation to the strengthening and confirmation of their Islamic beliefs and values. One of the outcomes of this family influence, evident in Raya, Rashida and Raja's stories was a sense of pride in their own and their family's accomplishments. In Raya's case, at a time when literacy was not routinely expected of girls, her mother saw her leadership potential and encouraged her reading and writing through learning the Quran.

Both Raya and Raja's mothers played an important role in developing and nurturing their respective moral and spiritual selves.

Their fathers also played a significant support role for both Raja and Rashida, providing encouragement for their education and, in Raja's case, ultimately trusting her with leading the family business. Such a role for a woman was not common at that time but Raja's potential, evident in her steadiness and strength, impressed her father. In Rashida's case she felt both protected and uplifted 'under the wing' of her father. The women felt uplifted because of family and valued learning from the previous generation and in many cases surpassed them in their leadership capacities and practices.

From an early stage they were recognized and supported as potential leaders mainly by family members and also by others. Recognition of Fatma's leadership potential was evident during her schooling where particular teachers gave her confidence in her abilities and helped develop her independence, traits that she would build on in later life. The educational authorities recognized Raja's skills and appointed her as a principal very early in her career, and the same authorities encouraged Rashida to enter the Ministry of Education. This recognition and support led to self efficacy and self recognition and an ongoing desire to build on and further develop that leadership potential.

In UAE society family responsibilities are of particular importance, both for immediate family (e.g. spouse and children) and for the extended family (brothers, sisters, cousins, parents etc). Each of our women leaders had been influenced by their own parents and it was clear that, for those with children, this influence was passed on. The immediate family dynamics differed for the five women and their stories indicated the different ways this played out. In each case the importance of spending time with family members was essential to who they were as individuals and it was here that different aspects of the relational qualities of their leadership were shown. The bonds of family relationships were strong and secure for each and consolidated their self knowledge and confidence in their relationships with others. Four of the women had children of their own and it was evident that just as they had been recognized as potential leaders by their parents they in turn looked for ways to encourage leadership in their own offspring. Raja for example prepared her children to enter the family business as they matured. As young adults the family members were very aware of their mothers' (and in Rashida's case, aunt's) knowledge and abilities as leaders. Thus an intergenerational continuity of leadership was both established, recognized, furthered and celebrated. Work-life balance was also maintained through the close friendship between Raja, Rashida, Rafia and Fatma. This friendship was forged in their educational experiences as young adults and through the intertwining of their career paths.

2   Realizing Their Own Leadership Potential and That of Others

An important element in their leadership was a deep knowledge of the content of their work, built up by their own approach to learning as a lifelong practice and their desire to continually extend their knowledge so that they could be more effective helping others to grow and develop. Such leadership practices resonated with situational (Hersey & Blanchard, 1993), transformational (Bass, 1997; Bass & Avolio, 1994; Burns, 1978); servant (Greenleaf, 2003; Spears, 1996), shared (Harris, 2005) and leading learning perspectives (Lambert, 2002). Their knowledge grew from childhood and family experiences and, for Rashida, Raja, Fatma and Rafia, was later strengthened by formal education. We noticed that each of the five women valued, and were committed to their own ongoing learning. The over-riding vision for these leaders was improving both themselves and the lives of others (Greenleaf, 2003) through their own lifelong learning and giving back to their students and society.

Their own professional learning was continuous and a core part of their leadership of others (Robinson, 2011). As they continued to learn during their careers, and to grow in professional knowledge and skills, and in their understanding of the practices that would lead to success in the classroom, they were better placed to influence increasing numbers of their teacher colleagues to engage in improved pedagogical practices (Burns, 1978; Dinham, 2016).

The concept of service to others was thus a clear purpose of their leadership (Greenleaf, 1970, 2003). They each had a clear sense of continuity and passed on knowledge and wisdom to the current generation with whom they worked. For Rashida, Raja, Fatma and Rafia there was a concurrent ability to identify leadership potential in others and to develop and support this through encouragement and dispositions of kindness, flexibility and respect for others. In addition, both Raya and Raja's values of stability and self discipline commanded respect from others. Again, these practices resonate with the way transformational leaders approach their work (Burns, 1978).

First and foremost these women were educational leaders and their purpose was leading learning for the betterment of themselves and others. For the four who were based in the compulsory education sector, student achievement was at the core of their leadership work. Their work was grounded in the 'leadership of learning' (Dinham, 2016; Hattie & Yates, 2014; Roberston & Timplerly, 2011), reflecting a deep understanding of the impact of leadership, professional learning and educational change (the latter of which was accelerating apace at the time they entered the UAE educational system as teachers and leaders). Their vision aligned with the growing expectations for change in education and their mission was to promulgate new content and innovative teaching strategies to help their colleagues to become better teachers and educators and thus impact on the success and achievement of their students.

The understanding of their own solid foundations kept them authentic and focused on their purpose in their leadership practices (Avolio & Gardner, 2005; Burns, 1978; Luthans & Youssef, 2004). Rashida, Raja, Fatima and Rafia have a very strong sense of who they are and yet they are able to go beyond their own ego to ensure that others' leadership potential is developed and realized. Their self knowledge is thus expressed through self*less*ness (Cameron, 2008; Greenleaf, 2003). They acknowledge the importance and significance of their own abilities and work towards developing others' leadership knowledge and skill (Lambert, 2002).

3 The Use of Relational Leadership Practices

Within their broad vision of contributing to their family and society each of the women brought a particular relational focus to their leadership work in their individual contexts (Lambert, 2002). Raya's focus was very much on family and community and ensuring that the values inherent in Islam and that were the 'glue' of community life, were passed on to younger members of society. Fatma's concern was related to effective communication; influencing others, negotiating with and persuading varied and different constituencies to help develop and shape *their* understanding of what was needed to improve education (Burns, 1978; Rost, 1991). Rashida and Rafia had a similar focus in some respects – that of leading by example and bringing innovative practices to their peers and colleagues in the education sector. They practised leadership as an interactive process of collaboration where authority and influence were shared (Rost, 1991). Although Raja had begun her leadership in a similar educational context her leadership had widened to a focus on the development of women in Arab society and to helping others understand it beyond the common stereotypes. These concepts and characteristics clearly align with a transformational leadership (Burns, 1978) perspective where the leader seeks to positively impact on the motivation, empowerment and moral purpose of organizational members (Bush, 2003; Gill, 2006; Rost, 1991). The attributes of relational and transformational leadership were demonstrated in the ways that these women used consultative and participative approaches and role-modelling to engage their constituents in creative and innovative processes as they collaborated towards shared goals (Rost, 1991). Their interpersonal skills enabled them to develop close relationships with those with whom they worked and to encourage them to invest in innovative practices and positive change (Burns, 1978; Hersey & Blanchard, 1993).

What was significant in the stories of each participant was the ways in which they built and led relationships with others (Cameron, 2008; Rost, 1991). Warmth, humour and kindness framed who they were as people and the way they interacted with others. Each of the women was personable and likable as a human being because of these dispositions. Despite the commonalities there were some additional personality attributes that distinguished the women from each other. For example, Raja and Raya were both private and very self disciplined. Raja was very measured in her interaction with others. Rashida, Fatma and Rafia exhibited courage, tenacity and perseverance in constantly moving forward their agendas of improving education and building capacity in their colleagues and co-workers.

Further evidence of relational skills was shown in the way the participants used respectful communication and negotiation in their interaction with others. When Raja first entered the business world she spent long hours visiting the factories and showrooms, assisting with day to day tasks and getting to know her employees, a practice which in turn encouraged their respect and loyalty (Spillane, Camburn, & Pareja, 2007). Similarly to Raja, Rashida, Fatma and Rafia honed their communication and negotiation skills early in their careers as they worked in school settings and during their ongoing career path in the Ministry of Education these skills became important to their success in building relationships with a much wider constituency including not only school personnel but also members of the educational authorities and in some cases the wider public. Rashida, for example, noted the sensitivity needed when visiting schools to identify areas for improvement and then negotiating with principals to convince them of the value of positive changes in teachers' work. Her strategy was to visit school sites frequently and talk 'face to face' as a colleague with principals and teachers. This horizontal relationship structure was used by all of the women, underpinning their views of the values of service to others, sharing and collegiality, and was an essential practice for the development of trust.

It was clear that all of the women had the ability to foster trust in others. Critical to their leadership was a knowledge of ways to relate to others that would lead to success. Raja, for example, knew what it was like to be an employee, so that when she moved from education to business and became an employer that earlier knowledge enabled her to understand and effectively relate to and lead the employees in the family companies. Rashida's work with the teachers was intentionally aimed at mentoring and coaching rather than a hierarchical model of critical evaluation and fault finding. Raya was trusted with the key role of passing on Islamic knowledge, values and traditions and as such was highly respected within the community.

At the core of their relational leadership approaches was a willingness to share leadership with others (Lambert, 2002; Cameron, 2008; Yousef-Morgan & Luthans, 2013; Rost, 1991), in order to encourage their colleagues to learn with and from them. Shared leadership has dual benefits. First, it allows the task of implementing educational change to be led more widely and thus have a higher likelihood of success. Secondly, over time, a new generation of leaders emerges from the mentoring and support of their more experienced colleagues. Both aspects of teacher leadership (Stephenson, 2011) were evident in the work of our four school based leaders.

Another feature is that they recognized that leadership development and becoming more effective as a leader takes hard work and effort. Their stories reflected this in various ways. Raya was often left with family responsibilities for long periods while her husband was at sea, and in a similar way Fatma's early widowhood also left her with comparable responsibilities. They both drew on an inner determination and resilience to continue their work. Hard work and effort was also evident in Raja's career development. After she moved into the business sector for example she was determined to know every aspect of the family business and thus worked in different sectors building her understanding and expertise. Her father warned her it would take ten years to 'learn the business,' advice that she questioned initially but in retrospect recognized as critical in helping her to gain a deep understanding of what was needed to continue successful development of the company. And as their careers developed Rafia, Fatma and Rashida took on leadership roles where they had demanding responsibilities that required flexibility and ability to adapt. While acknowledging these demands, their drive and passion for their work enabled them to cope with varied challenging situations. These practices link to situational leadership (Hersey, 1985; Hersey & Blanchard, 1993) where the focus is on the leader's ability to 'read' a situation, including the needs of constituents and to adapt and change if needed.

The concept of servant leadership and stewardship (Greenleaf, 1977, 2003) permeated the leadership work of our participants. Here the leader's focus is not on their own interests but rather in commitment to the growth of others and to the building of a sustainable and ongoing community among those who he/she serves. The concept of service to others and to the UAE that underpinned each woman's leadership work, is one which has strong roots in Arab culture (Sarayrah, 2004). Echoing Sarayrah's (2004) points, modern versions of servant leadership emphasize mentoring, listening skills, empathy, vision and foresight by a leader whose integrity and personal values command trust and respect. These practices were clearly demonstrated by our participants. Other leadership dispositions that were consistent in the practices of the five women were courage, the willingness to take risks at times, and a preparedness to face up to and take on life challenges.

Sarayrah (2004) outlines particular leadership practices of the Caliph that are replicated in the leadership work of our five women; for example, the ability to listen and accept critical feedback, the ability to plan and organise, the ability to involve others in decision-making through collaborative, consultative discussion, the ability to empathise with others and the ability to effect change and deal with problems. Also underpinning their leadership practice was the disposition of respect. Self respect was developed in each by the positive relationships and support they had received from their early years and this in turn lead to a clear sense of respect for others with whom they worked. Confidence and courage were also key values demonstrated by Rafia, Rashida, Fatma and Raja. The ability to be calm in their interaction with others was evident in Raya, Rafia and Raja. Humility (e.g. Raya and Rashida) and kindness (e.g. Raya, Rashida and Rafia) were two of the related values emerging from the analysis. The values and inclusive dispositions exhibited through the participants' transpersonal (Knights, 2011, 2017) and relational practices resonate with more humanist and post industrial leadership perspectives and models (Komives, Lucas, & McMahon, 2007).

4   Conclusion

The preceding chapters narrate the lived leadership experiences of five unique women in Dubai. The stories span a broad range of years and thus capture the essence of changes and transitions in the culture, community and the UAE during that time.

The story of Raya, the senior participant, captures her leadership during a quieter more traditional and stable time in the UAE and is clearly grounded in family values. The stories of the other younger four also reveal values driven leadership practices. However, due to the time of rapid development of the country, they were additionally provided opportunities that were relationally motivated and change-oriented. They offered a 'trail-blazing' vision and purpose to make a difference to education and to the lives and achievement of teachers, families and children. The individual stories highlight particular characteristics and lived experiences that are unique to each participant but together they reveal mutual themes that link their leadership work across common patterns, providing insight into the ways their leadership was influenced by their values and Islamic faith. The critical significance of parental and family encouragement and support is not to be underestimated. The five women were steadfast in their sense of self and purpose which enabled them to understand their own leadership potential but also that of others. Finally, building relational trust enabled them to realize that potential fulfilling their essential purpose as leaders of learning.

The narration of the stories is significant in that the researchers were granted the opportunity to meet with and learn about the lives of the participants in ways that are rarely privileged to outsiders. The stories are significant in the way that they speak to intergenerational concerns, look both backward and forward to highlight key leadership matters and underscore the cross-generational importance of values. There is much to be learned about successful leadership through reflecting on the journeys that each of them have made and continue to make together with their individual values and practices and their collective impact on those whom they have led and lead.

The leaders of the UAE have long recognized the integral role women leaders play in the development of their country and have recently begun to celebrate this each year on Emirati Women's Day. The year 2017–2018 has been entitled the Year of Zayed, underscoring the leadership values, including his support for women, of the late H.H. Sheikh Zayed, the 'father of the nation.' His views resonate in the words of H.H. Sheikh Mohammed bin Zayed Al Nahyan who stated that "Women are the heart of the nation and integral to its progress. They're capable and empowered leaders who can take our nation to new heights" ("Leaders congratulate Emirati women," 2017, para. 6). Our participants are such women.

References

Avolio, B. J., & Gardner, W. L. (2005). Authentic leadership development: Getting to the root of positive forms of leadership. *The Leadership Quarterly, 16*, 315–338.

Bass, B. M. (1997). *The ethics of transformational leadership* (Kellogg Leadership Studies Project, Transformational Leadership Working Papers). College Park, MD: The James MacGregor Burns Academy of Leadership Press.

Bass, B. M., & Avolio, B. J. (Eds.). (1994). *Improving organizational effectiveness through transformational leadership.* Thousand Oaks, CA: Sage Publications.

Burns, J. M. (1978). *Leadership.* New York, NY: Harper & Row.

Bush, T. (2003).Theory and practice in educational management. In T. Bush, M. Coleman, & M. Thurlow (Eds.), *Leadership and strategic management in South African schools.* London: Commonwealth Secretariat.

Cameron, K. S. (2008). *Positive leadership: Strategies for extraordinary performance.* San Francisco, CA: Berrett-Koehler Publishers.

Dinham, S. (2016). *Leading learning and teaching.* Camberwell: ACER Press.

Gill, R. (2006). *Theory and practice of leadership.* Thousand Oaks, CA: Sage Publications.

Greenleaf, R. K. (1970). *The servant as leader* (pp. 1–37). Indianapolis, IN: The Robert K. Greenleaf Center.

Greenleaf, R. K. (1977). *Servant leadership: A journey into the nature of legitimate power and greatness.* New York, NY: Paulist Press.

Greenleaf, R. K. (2003). *The servant-leader within: A transformative path.* New York, NY: Paulist Press.

Harris, A. (2005). Distributed leadership. In B. Davies (Ed.), *The essentials of school leadership.* London: Paul Chapman.

Hattie, J., & Yates, G. (2014). *Visible learning and the science of how we learn.* Oxford: Routledge.

Hersey, P. (1985). *The situational leader.* New York, NY: Warner Books.

Hersey, P., & Blanchard, K. H. (1993). *Management of organizational behavior: Utilizing human resources.* Englewood Cliffs, NJ: Prentice Hall.

Knights, J. (2011). *The invisible elephant & the pyramid treasure.* London: Tomorrows Company. Retrieved from http://www.leadershape.biz/invisible-elephant

Knights, J. (2017). *Ethical leadership: How to develop ethical leaders* (White Paper). Retrieved June 01, 2017, from https://www.routledge.com/posts/9951

Komives, S. R., Lucas, N., & McMahon, T. R. (2013). *Exploring leadership: For college students who want to make a difference* (3rd ed.). San Francisco, CA: Jossey-Bass.

Lambert, L. (2002). *Leadership capacity for lasting school improvement.* Alexandria, VA: Association for Supervision and Curriculum Development.

Leaders congratulate Emirati women. (2017, August 27). *Gulf News.* Retrieved from http://gulfnews.com/news/uae/government/leaders-congratulate-emirati-women-1.2081011

Luthans, F., & Avolio, B. J. (2003). Authentic leadership: A positive developmental approach. In K. S. Cameron, J. E. Dutton, & R. E. Quinn (Eds.), *Positive organizational scholarship* (pp. 241–261). San Francisco, CA: Barrett-Koehler.

Luthans, F., & Youssef, C. M. (2004). Human, social, and now positive psychological capital management: Investing in people for competitive advantage. *Organizational Dynamics, 33*(2), 143–160.

Robertson, J., & Timperley, S. (Eds.). (2011). *Leadership and learning.* London: Sage Publications.

Robinson, V. (2011). *Student-centred leadership*. San Francisco, CA: Jossey-Bass.

Rost, J. C. (1991). *Leadership for the twenty-first century*. Westport, CT: Praeger.

Sarayrah, Y. K. (2004). Servant leadership in the Bedouin-Arab culture. *Global Virtual Ethics Review, 5*(3), 58–79.

Shah, S. (2006). Educational leadership: An Islamic perspective. *British Educational Research Journal, 32*(3), 363–385.

Spears, L. (1996). Reflections on Robert K. Greenleaf and servant-leadership. *Leadership & Organization Development Journal, 17*, 33–35.

Spillane, J. P., Camburn, E. M., & Pareja, A. S. (2007). Taking a distributed perspective to the school principal's workday. *Leadership and Policy in Schools, 6*(1), 103–125. doi:10.1080/15700760601091200

Stephenson, L. (2011). *Conducting an investigation into the nature of teacher leadership and its impact on school improvement*. Abu Dhabi: Abu Dhabi Education Council-Research Office.

Youssef-Morgan, C. M., & Luthans, F. (2013). *Positive leadership: Meaning and application across cultures* (Paper 127). Lincoln, NE: Management Department Faculty Publications. Retrieved from http://digitalcommons.unl.edu/managementfacpub/127

Glossary

abaya   a loose-fitting full-length robe worn by Emirati women
adhan   call to prayer
aiwa   yes
al meryeihana   swing
al saglah   game played by tossing and catching small stones
al qhararaeef   bedtime stories
Alhamdulillah   thanks to Allah
areesh   dwelling with walls covered in palm fronds
bajela   beans
balaleet   a sweet vermicelli and egg dish
baba   father
Bismillah, Rahmane Rahim   in the name of Allah, the Beneficent, the Merciful
burqa   a loose veil covering part of the face, worn by Muslim women
dalla   coffee pot
fanar   lantern
habibti   term on endearment
hadith   a written collection of things said and done by the Prophet Muhammed
Haj   special pilgrimage to Mecca
harees   dish of boiled, cracked, or coarsely-ground wheat, mixed with meat
henna   a plant dye used for decorating the body and colouring hair
iftar   breaking the fast in Ramadan
khemeer   bread
mabrook   congratulations
maghrib   prayer (4th of the five daily prayers; offered just at sunset)
majlis   room in home where visitors are welcomed
manaz   cradle
mash'allah   a phrase used to show appreciation or blessing for a person or
    happening
mirfaa   a wooden holder for the Holy Quran
mutawa'a   member of a community responsible for teaching the Holy Quran
    to children
nokhada   ship captain
shayla   head scarf
tanoor   earth oven
Taraweeh prayer   extra prayers performed by Muslims at night in the Islamic
    month of Ramadan

thobe   an ankle-length dress worn by women in the UAE
umi   mother
umm al lal   children's game where 'mother' protects her 'babies' from a 'wolf'